Majesty
IN MOTION

Creating an ENCOURAGEMENT
Culture in All Your RELATIONSHIPS

Stewart Brown, D. Min.

MAJESTY IN MOTION
Creating an Encouragement Culture in All Your Relationships

ISBN-10: 1-926676-45-9
ISBN-13: 978-1-926676-45-6

Printed in Canada.

Printed by Word Alive Press
131 Cordite Road, Winnipeg, MB R3W 1S1
www.wordalivepress.ca
WORD ALIVE PRESS
Just Write!

I dedicate this book to
Sandra
my wife, life partner, and
chief encourager on this planet

ENDORSEMENTS

A must read for anyone wanting to experience the transformative power of God! Stewart Brown has woven together years of personal experience, astute observation of people, and Scripture to present an engaging, easily understandable antidote to much of the joylessness, frustration, and struggle many people experience. He makes a compelling case for focusing on others through becoming an intentional encourager. But he knows that active engagement with God comes first, then comes engagement with others. Only by moving outside ourselves can we experience joy. Brown gives practical suggestions on how to do that. The Study Guide leads the reader to deeper understanding, either on one's own or, preferably, in company with others.

MEL FINLAY
National Director
Nation At Prayer

Dr. Brown... has encouraged me so many times. Learn from the once discouraged who has become an instrument of encouragement!

DR. SADIRI TIRA (D.MIN. D.MISS.)
Senior Associate for Diasporas
Lausanne Committee for World evangelization

Let's be honest. If you are a human being living on planet earth, you are a liar! We lie to each other and ourselves daily; even those who consider themselves full-blown, saved-by-the-blood– and bound-for-eternity Christians who have given their lives to Jesus Christ. Yes, we lie constantly. Not necessarily in a malicious or deceitful way, but often because we don't want to burden others or just because we're too tired of talking about it. Our lie is offered when asked at church, work or home, how we're doing. The answer all too often is "fine," when in truth we are desperately hurting inside and need love and encouragement.

Stewart Brown is a modern day Barnabas—an encourager!

His book, *Majesty in Motion,* is a searing lance that breaks through our defenses to point out that we both need encouragement and can give encouragement. And he shows us both aspects clearly, precisely and practically, all the while bringing us closer to God.

With clear biblical teaching, Dr. Brown challenges the liar in us, urging us to complete honesty with ourselves and before God. And then he shows us how, by embracing God's love, majesty, and holiness we can be encouraged by Him and then move beyond our own circumstances to encourage and impact the lives of others. He intersperses personal experiences with biblical illustrations and ties them all together in one profound concept— encouragement! You need it, I need it; you can give it, I can give it. Stewart guides us clearly though such topics as joy, patience, developing healthy relationships, removing our masks, freedom from addiction, forgiveness, and practicing encouragement, among others.

He wraps the sound teaching in the spiritual and theoretical realm with practical help. Each chapter ends with no-nonsense guidance and questions for individuals and small groups to consider and then put into practice.

v

Majesty in Motion offers a fresh and encouraging take on a subject all too often neglected in Christian circles. Read the book. Be encouraged. And go out and encourage others.

BARRIE DOYLE, APR
Author, Broadcaster,
Public Relations Consultant, Professor

ACKNOWLEDGEMENTS

It is impossible to really live life without real encouragement. It is also true that this book could not have been written without three special encouragers inspiring me to cross the 'finish line!' Sandra, my amazing wife, has been my chief encourager from the day we were married. Her corrections and modifications in my spelling, grammar and other details have given me confidence to submit this book for publishing. Our son, Tim, spent considerable time reviewing and editing chapters of the book. His wife, Joelle, also contributed insights and suggestions. I have experienced God as my intentional encourager through their love and contributions.

Although they were not directly involved in this book, our other sons David and Mark, daughters-in-law, Krysten and Lola, and our granddaughters, Anna Kate and Alberta Jean, have each contributed to my joy and encouragement which I seek to share with you, my readers.

FOREWORD

I have read that forewords in books are to be written by *those who matter,*[*] and I have to admit that when I was asked to write one for this book I questioned whether or not I adequately represented those people. I suppose I do matter very much to the man who wrote this book, as he is my father. Over the years, I have seen him embody the very qualities he writes about. Given that he is my dad, you might really wonder if I could say otherwise, but the truth is that for years I've seen him encourage others, and seek to instil that same passion for caring in those he encourages. This is his passion, driven by his faith and love.

Now, before you go skipping off to read the book, pause a spell and let me tell you a bit about what it is that you'll be reading. Because you'll be there a little while. Best to know the lay of the land, so to speak, so you won't get lost.

The book you'll be reading has been a long time in coming. Decades perhaps. You're not simply reading the project of someone who set out to write a book, or simply put pen to paper. You're going to read the passionate exhortations of a man who

[*] http://museinks.blogspot.com

believes well and truly that intentional encouragement matters, and that when you find yourself agreeing with this, your life will change.

We are not talking a quick, flashy change, offered up for two easy payments (with more, if you'll call in the next ten minutes). Nothing here is like cheap grace, with a proffered benefit bereft of sacrifice. Choosing to be an intentional encourager might not come easily; it might even be very difficult for you. But I believe, as Stewart believes, that it is important *that it come to you.* This is not a new thought, but its value doesn't lie in innovation. It lies in truth.

I may not be someone who matters in some ways, but I can tell you that what you read can alter your thoughts, and through your thoughts, your actions, and through your actions, your life. In the end, I really hope that you enjoy this book and that it will bless and rejuvenate you.

TIMOTHY BROWN

TABLE OF CONTENTS

INTRODUCTION

Perhaps you long to discover some way to escape or rise above the mess, pain, and pressures of life. Even if you are young, it may dawn on you that the overwhelming numbers of choices in your life are just more of the same. A realization grows in you that real lasting fulfillment in your life is only possible by rising above the common and predictable routine of daily living. But how can you rise to a higher level? Is it not true that you want more than money, a house, a car, and super-stressful commutes on highways or city streets?

Yes, there is a way! This way is contained within two incredible words that are packed with meaning and power— **intentional encouragement**. Encouragement means far more than feeling good. It is more than the exchange of superficial greetings that make someone feel good for a moment. Such action does nothing to address that need deep inside your heart that cripples your capacity to really live, create, and make a lasting impact on the lives of others. Encouragement is the result of a dynamic connection and intimate union of your heart with the heart of God. This union with God will motivate and empower you to fulfill His eternal purposes for your life. To be encouraged is to experience the transformative power of God, which gives you the **courage** to be and act according to God's eternal purpose for your life. The basis of this book is deeply rooted in the many amazing characteristics of encouragement revealed in the Bible. In particular, there are three life principles by which you can live a profoundly fulfilling life in community with others around you. They can help transform those around you— your spouse, family, fellow worker, neighbor, and those in your local church.

Real lasting encouragement is **intentional**! To encourage someone so that they are inspired to align their character with that of Jesus requires you to be intentional in your thoughts and actions. It is not an automatic routine. It requires you to grow in intimacy with God and in sensitivity to the people around you. It requires you to be willing to pray for, understand, and lead another closer to God. Only then can find life, joy, and a transformative peace that will make their lives count now and for eternity! It means that you focus on who you are becoming first and foremost, and not on what you do. What you do must flow out of what and who you are becoming. Intentional encouragement requires a new mindset focused on **relationships** instead of activities. It is based on the principle of Jesus, who said to His first disciples: *"Freely you have received, freely give"* (Matthew 10:8). It is as basic as breathing. Living requires breathing, or receiving air into your lungs and giving it back out. Whatever you have received from God, whatever blessing, do not hold tightly to it, acting like a child, saying "It's mine!" Whatever you receive from God, be willing to give or share it in His name.

Introduction

Surprised by God

Early in the morning, I jumped out of bed, dressed, left my hotel room, and headed out into the nearby woods in Banff National Park in Alberta, Canada. I wanted to do a little running, but mostly brisk walking so that I could breathe the fresh air, listen to the sounds, drink in the soaring mountain beauty—and in that context, to connect more deeply with God. After arriving on the edge of the town of Banff, I walked into the woods and up over a small hill. Arriving at the top of the hill, I spotted three beautiful deer.

A most amazing experience began. The deer did not run, but looked at me. Even as I walked closer, they did not run. I could almost touch them. One deer appeared to desire a closer inspection of me. Just hours earlier, I had had some trouble sleeping because something was on my mind. Suddenly, I was surprised by God. In those magnificent deer, I saw the beauty of God! The deer closest to me blinked its eye and I received it as a "wink" from my Creator and Savior. God was communicating to me—an impression in my heart that said, "Stewart, it's all right. I love you and forgive you. I embrace you with my grace and power." Twice, I left the deer and returned to that place. The deer remained there.

I felt like I was on holy ground. Even though God lives in my heart through my faith relationship with his Son, Jesus Christ, I knew that this was a special sanctuary of God where I had a special transforming encounter with Him. A psalm came to my mind and I prayed God's Word back to Him:

> As the deer pants for streams of water,
> so my souls pants for you, O God.
> My soul thirsts for God, for the Living God
> Where can I go and meet with God? (...)

Why are you downcast, O my soul?
Why so disturbed within me?
Put your hope in God,
for I will yet praise Him,
My Savior and my God. (...)
Deep calls to deep...
(Psalm 42:1-2,5,7a)

As I called out to God, I prayed that He would increase my thirst for Him. My desire for God had to come first. I knew that my life could then be a transforming influence on all my other relationships. I would have greater understanding, wisdom, and love in dealing with the people and events that daily life presented to me.

As I recalled Psalm 42, I suddenly became aware of a water brook behind me! I saw God smiling at me through the deer that morning. I sensed His welcoming, affirming, strengthening embrace that empowered me to touch the hearts of others that day.

That encounter continues to inspire my heart. This is God's purpose—to instill real encouragement in me, revealing His **majesty** to me so that He can reveal His majesty through me. On that day in Banff, I witnessed **the majesty of God in motion**! This is God's plan for you—expressing His encouragement, His majesty, through your unique personality. God's majesty is revealed through the purposeful motions of your life. Continue reading in great expectation that God will enable you to *experience* and *express* the transforming power of intentional encouragement.

THE WAY TO JOY

In this book, we will look at the experience and expression of joy—the real foundation to lasting encouragement. Joy arises out of a personal growing faith relationship with Jesus Christ as Savior and director of my life. It is not automatic, but a process that continues all through my life on this earth. This requires me to live with my focus on God. It is on this basis that I then desire to see others as God sees them. My priority is not on myself, but on others as God directs me. The more I grow in character-likeness to Jesus, the more joy will overflow through my life and inspire others to move closer to Jesus. Joy is the result of committing my life to fulfilling God's supreme purposes in me. It requires an intentional effort— an enormous effort on my part—to pay whatever the cost and *follow hard after Jesus. The older I get, the greater the urgency to live God's way.*

> For the "2nd half" [of your life] to be better than the first, you must make the choice to step out of the safety of auto pilot.[i]

I believe that this is possible if I am willing to live *all* of my life realizing and accepting that I was created by God, so that in (faith) community with others, God can display His awesome glory! Now is the time for you to make the most important choice of your life. It means that you choose short-term pain for long-term gain. If you will seek God and read the Bible on a daily basis, God will use the Bible as the raw material to form Christ-like character in you. In the process of living with God everyday, you will begin to realize that the most important thing is who you are becoming. What you do will flow out of what you are becoming in the person and power of Jesus, the Son of God.

PART ONE

THE LIFE OF ENCOURAGEMENT

CHAPTER ONE
A New Paradigm of Living

SEEKING FIRST TO UNDERSTAND, THEN TO INSPIRE

The door of the plane was mere seconds away from closing! A huge amount of time had gone into the planning of this trip. I was about to meet several groups of people, with whom I would have times of intense discussion. But, at this point, my mind was not on those matters. Instead, I was determined to pray for the person who might sit next to me on the plane. I could have just focused on myself, but I wanted to escape from the mindset that says 'Me first.' I wanted God to work through me to have an impact on the life of the person I was yet to meet.

Just before the door closed, a young twenty-something man walked in and sat on my right side. In my prayer, I asked God to draw that person to Himself by placing his personal faith in Jesus as his Savior. I prayed that whatever his needs, God would reveal Himself to that person and empower him to see that his entire life could be transformed by allowing God to work in his heart from the inside out. I greeted him and then went back to praying and reading. We both took a brief nap.

Halfway through the flight, I initiated a conversation with Paul (not his real name).

God answered my prayer of faith for Paul. He led me to respond with grace and to ask the appropriate questions in an attitude of loving concern. God had obviously prepared Paul's heart. He told me about his dream of becoming a teacher. In our conversation, I told him that in a career of teaching, attitude and relationships were very important. But, I said, the most important relationship that you need is your relationship with God. Out of your relationship with God, you can then teach much more effectively with diligence, love, and care.

Paul suddenly opened up and expressed a great desire to know more about God. I gave him some literature explaining how God sent His Son, Jesus, to earth so that Jesus could give His life as Savior for all who would trust him by faith. In my carry-on bag, there was only one book of the Bible, a Gospel of John. I gave it to Paul and explained how his life could be forever transformed by rejecting sin and selfishness and inviting Jesus to 'occupy' his heart and direct the rest of his life. Before the end of the flight, I invited him to put his trust in Jesus. I do not act like this on a regular basis, but I was sensitive enough to the Spirit of God that this was the right action to take. Amazingly, there on the plane, Paul prayed to invite Jesus to take over his heart and life. We prayed audibly to thank God for his gift of eternal life. Other passengers could hear our words.

Who knows how many were made aware of the call of God that day because I chose to depart from my old self-centered paradigm or pattern of thinking and put God and others first? In the old, more common paradigm of encouragement, a per-

4

son thinks that it is all about what you do for someone in your workplace. They think, 'If I smile, say good morning, and say something nice, then I have been encouraging to my colleague. If I offer to cut the grass for my neighbor, then I have really done well—the neighbor must really be impressed.' Some think that if they are friendly and greet a visitor, that person will then want to return to their church. Surely, they have been encouraged. But outward actions combined with visible results still do not ensure that a person has been really encouraged or profoundly impacted in a positive, lasting way. Many organizations, churches, and businesses tend to assume that employees and staff are doing well when the outcomes show more people in attendance, more customers, and better financial results. The old definition of encouragement focuses on activities and measurable results while ignoring the inner needs, struggles, and dreams of the persons who serve, minister, and bring about the visible results.

The danger is to think that the church is successful because it has the appropriate personnel, with the right mix of abilities, achieving desired visible results. We can be so focused on our abilities that we fail to seek an intimate relationship with God. We can be so eager to complete a task that we miss *kairos* moments of opportunity to connect with a needy person along the way. The old way of encouraging is to emphasize connecting with a maximum number of people but neglecting to deeply touch even one. It is quantity over quality. All too common is the tendency to pursue one's own agenda and task while totally ignoring the persons around us until a problem, conflict, or disaster emerges. We can work for years with the same person and suddenly discover that we do not really know her at all until she explodes, or conflict erupts, enlarging a matter far beyond its scope or importance. We are shocked by this because we never took time and effort to walk deeper into the life of the other.

NEW PARADIGM

In contrast to the above, a new paradigm requires the practice of real **intentional** encouragement. The old idea of encouragement emphasizes the sharing of activity *with* another person. But the new paradigm of encouragement emphasizes **relationship** with another person and the desire to see into the heart of him or her. It starts with our journey deeper into the heart of God. No longer are you satisfied with superficial surface contacts with people. In this new paradigm, you want to deeply know God. Out of this dynamic union with God, you can now have both the desire and the ability to more deeply understand the other person. This other person may be your spouse, your child, parent, or colleague in the workplace.

Long ago, King David sought God with overflowing tears as he pleaded for forgiveness and restoration of his heart with the heart of God. Once his heart was restored to God, he received the ability to inspire and influence others in connecting with God by a transforming faith relationship (Psalm 51:12-13). David understood that, if he grew deeper into God, he would become more intentional in being sensitive to others around him, seeking to understand their hearts, and striving to meet their needs by allowing God to work through him. This is encouragement that more profoundly impacts a person and leads them to lasting change from the inside out.

The need for such change is obvious! You may be 'falling through the cracks' and hurting deep inside, unnoticed, because co-leaders in your church are too busy to really notice. Your co-worker may be focused first on her job or on increasing favor with her boss and miss even the most obvious signs. When this happens, misunderstandings increase between you and the flow of progress may soon be screeching to a halt. Many of us cannot see with our eyes wide open. In the words of a movie title, we walk or run around with our *eyes wide shut!*

The keys were nowhere to be found. I was frustrated and started to complain. What the heck happened to those keys? I can't believe this.

"Why don't you look?" Sandra responded. "Stewart, open your eyes. Take the time to look."

I didn't want to look. If I couldn't see them instantly, they had disappeared. Rather than take time to reflect on what had caused them to go missing, how I might find them, and correct the problem so that I would know where to get them the next time, I chose to complain. I would either put myself down or blame someone else. What was I doing wrong? I was looking at the problem, but not **intentionally** *taking time to think, see, or reflect on the need for correction in me and the opportunity to bless my wife rather than blame her.*

In our Western culture, we run around trying to multitask—talk on the cell phone, eat a sandwich, and apply make-up, all while attempting to drive safely on the road! Many people are so fixated on grabbing quickly what they want that they will run you over in the process without knowing you are there. You may be overloaded and over-stressed. The last thing you need is to get knocked down or ignored. You need someone to take the time to help you to see, understand, and inspire you closer to God. You need someone who has been transformed by God to respect you as a valued human being specially created by God. Such a person is needed to help you 'surface' the deepest needs of your heart and inspire you to draw closer to God through a faith relationship with Jesus.

IGNORED AT IKEA

The new way, the real way of **genuine** encouragement, is obviously needed in our culture. One recent experience at our IKEA location confirmed this need.

It was Saturday morning at IKEA. We had just purchased our big breakfast for just $1.00. The next step was for me to walk in line to the area for condiments and beverages. Mere seconds before I could reach for the hot water dispenser, about a half dozen people jumped in front of me to grab ketchup or mustard. Not one of them could wait even thirty more seconds. They wanted it now! *It shocked me that they totally ignored me. It was as if it was open space without anyone in their path. This is the amazing thing. No one looked at me. No one even politely said, 'Excuse me' Is it then surprising that so many others are guilty of the same self-focus?*

In intentional encouragement, God calls you to live with a constant awareness of Him in your daily life. It is out of that awareness and deep connection with him that you are called by God to live with a growing sensitivity to lonely, needy, and struggling persons all around you. Being really encouraged and living out a life of encouragement means imitating Jesus who *"saw the crowds [and] had compassion on them"* (Matthew 9:36). This is living the life that God intends for you. Live like Jesus. It means not ignoring the person near me at work, or next door, but **intentionally** seeking to understand that person so that, by the Spirit of God, you can be the instrument through which God fills a need in his or her life. Imagine the incredible impact this would have in your family, workplace, club, or church if each of us learned to live this way. But it starts with me. It starts with you. In the Bible, God provides the secret of living with joy and fulfillment when, through Paul the Apostle, He calls you to live this way:

> Wherever you are, whatever you do, don't ignore people you meet. Put them first. Treat each of them as valuable persons. Even as you connect with that person, desire God's very best for them. In doing this, you will begin receiving God's best for you. (Philippians 2:3-4, paraphrased)

Intentional encouragement requires me to see you as God sees you. If I treat my wife Sandra this way, she will grow into the beautiful woman God intends her to be. If I treat my children this way, they will blossom into men and women of Christ-like character, both strong and sensitive (tender) towards others. If I see the men and women in my workplace as unique individuals created by God, I'll look beyond their outward appearance or rough language *and inspire them to stop, reflect, and become productive employees that benefit all of us, our customers, and the whole community.* To act like this is to be in tune or in sync with the Spirit of God. Intentional encouragement requires God to be leading your life so "keep in step with the (Holy) Spirit" (Galatians 5:25).

9

PUMPED UP AND READY TO GO!

Real encouragement has three essential parts. To live a life of joy, peace, and fulfillment, and to achieve your greatest God-given potential, you need to experience all three and then give them all to others.

The first part of encouragement is **strengthening the heart**. *"And Saul's son Jonathan went to David at Horesh and helped him find strength in God"* (1 Samuel 23:16). I find this to be one of the most powerful verses in the Bible. The Hebrew word for "find strength" means to experience or receive strength in my heart. David had been discouraged—feeling weak in mind, spirit, and body—hardly able to face and succeed in any life challenge at this point. But Jonathan helped David to regain deep inner strength to face and win over even challenges that threatened his very life. In Psalm 10:17, God is seen as the one who encourages or gives strength to the hearts of those who trust in Him.

Our family spent much time camping with a five-person tent. That was the best we could afford as our three sons were growing up. Vivid memories exist of getting out the air mattress and pumping laboriously. Sometimes I would make progress only to let some of the air accidentally escape. But the aim was a comfortable night's sleep, so I kept on pumping. Once it had sufficient air, that mattress worked like a charm! It fully served its intended purpose. Intentional encouragement is like this. Once God has 'pumped' strength into my heart and revived my inner spirit, I desire to 'pump air' or strength into the heart of my friend or neighbor. Imagine the joy of 'pumping air into the deflated spirit of a discouraged person every day of your life.

*That is God's plan for you—this is **intentional living**. It is **joy-motivated living!***

When I feel encouraged—that is, really encouraged—even though my circumstances may not have greatly changed, my heart feels stronger, able to withstand and act with purpose in any situation. 'To encourage' means to *speak to the heart* (al-lebab).[ii] When God speaks to your heart, you can (by His Spirit) speak to the heart of someone weakened by the battles of daily life.

The hearts of people in the day of the Hebrew prophet Elijah were weakened by excessive sinful living. They seemed incapable of making an intelligent decision. They had been in one of those ruts in life—existing, but not really living. In a showdown on Mount Carmel, Elijah issues a clear challenge to his people:

"How long are you going to waver between two opinions?" (1 Kings 18:21)

The word 'waver' has the Hebrew sense of 'limp'—like a mattress without air. It means without form and without use—a mental, emotional, and spiritual condition that makes the heart weak and the person incapable of living with a purpose and of blessing others around him.

The second part of encouragement is **coming along side to help**. Before returning to heaven, Jesus promised His disciples to ask God the Father to He send another *counselor* or *comforter* (John 14:16). The term *counselor* means "one who is called to one's side or to one's aid."[iii] That requires you to seek intimacy with God. The Bible says that if you draw near to God, He will draw near to you (James 4:8). Let God come alongside you. Start every day by seeking God first. Be willing to pay whatever the cost to resist temptation, and tune out other competing voices and trashy useless information. Let the Bible always be your lifeline to seek and receive from God and let Jesus really be the director of your life everyday. If you belong to a local church, imitate Paul and Silas of the first century Christian church. Whenever you speak, intend your words to encourage or strengthen those who hear you (Acts 15:32). Before you come alongside some other person, you need intimacy with God *and* the willingness to get closer to that person. Your purpose must be to better understand that person—her needs and dreams. The more you understand a person and demonstrate a willingness to help him or her, the more likely you are to be that encourager coming alongside. The recipient of this genuine heart encouragement can then go on to deeply impact others and help change your whole community. That is the plan of God.

Melissa Mills, a young teenaged girl, faced a life-threatening situation. Initially triggered by a virus, her heart became enlarged and failed to properly pump her blood. Faced with the prospect of death, doctors began preparing Melissa for a heart transplant. While she waited, doctors implanted an artificial heart (called the Berlin Heart) in her body. The Berlin Heart was placed alongside Melissa's own diseased heart. An amazing thing happened! After a while, Melissa's own weakened heart began to regain strength with the help of the Berlin heart placed next to it. As Melissa's own heart grew stronger, the Berlin heart was 'turned down' more and more—until the diseased heart fully recovered. Then, the Berlin heart was taken away.[iv]

Melissa's story illustrates the second essential part of intentional encouragement—the will and ability you have to come alongside another person, providing them with a listening ear, sacrificial spirit, and compassionate attitude. When you have truly encouraged that person, he or she can then go on to strengthen someone else in your church, group, or organization.

The third part of encouragement is to **draw or inspire forward**. The Bible describes the great abilities and gifts of a man named Apollos who was encouraged and consistently inspired by fellow Christians to keep making progress, to grow and maximize his giftedness in glorifying God and empowering others to do the same (Acts 18:27). In the first century church, a wise, experienced and aging Paul pours out his life to draw out the best and inspire a young, rather timid man named Timothy. He challenges him to develop the focus of a soldier, the patience of a farmer, and the discipline of an athlete who is aiming for the 'gold medal' (2 Timothy 2:1-7).

Verdun Matts was a man who acted like a father to me. In addition to being a successful businessman, Verd also became youth director of a large youth ministry at my old home church, The Peoples' Church, in Toronto, Canada. He was passionate, gracious, wise, and patient in his ministry to us and with youth like me for many years. He and his wife Lorraine opened their hearts and their home continuously, or whenever any of us needed counsel or encouragement. Just before his death in his early 80s, Verd was still communicating to youth! He is one crucial reason why I am still in active Christian ministry today.

Verd was one encourager who truly inspired me forward into a closer relationship with God and into a deeper love for others in need. The secret of his influence was his willingness to understand a person before he encouraged them. He was never too busy to listen, learn, and lift anyone in need. He constantly reminded me that all of my life was to be lived within the gracious loving embrace of God. He would say, "Stewart, keep marching forward under the banner of Jesus Christ—don't give up; don't be afraid."

Verd was there when I needed him. He brought strength to my fearful, timid spirit and inspired me forward by his Christlike example. He was a man in motion displaying the majesty of God through his life. Encouragement is just that—the majesty of God in motion through the dynamic of lives passionate for Him!

Practical Steps for Individuals and Small Groups

1. What happens to spouses in a marriage, children in a family, members in a church, or employees in a workplace when they are discouraged?
2. What is **encouragement**?
3. What is **discouragement**?
4. Check the listed characteristics of the old paradigm (pattern, mindset) of encouragement. Are you living in the **old** paradigm?
5. Look carefully at the list for the new paradigm. Are you living in the **new** paradigm? If not, are you willing to take the necessary steps to get there?
6. What difference could this make in your marriage, family, church, or community?
7. How would you describe your personal journey in life? Are you experiencing God by being **transformed by** Him and not merely **informed about** Him?
8. Do you have a daily time set aside for God? How would you describe it? What benefits, insights, and/or needed corrections are you receiving? Record these in a daily journal. If you cannot name one insight or convicting truth that God has taught you this week, then your "daily time" with God is either too shallow or nonexistent.

9. The key to having an effective time with God is to **memorize** verses which inspire and impact you. When He speaks to you through a verse, memorize it. Write it out and carry it with you that day. Prayerfully ask God to give you one other person with whom you can share that verse. This will connect and motivate you more to live it out.

10. Review the three parts of intentional encouragement. Identify someone whom you can strengthen, help, and inspire in a) your family, b) your church, and c) your workplace or community.

11. Prayerfully look for and secure an accountable, encouraging partner. Agree to meet at least once a week with that person to discuss, practice, and reinforce the above principles of encouragement. Affirm, inspire, and challenge each other, drawing each other forward in Christ-like maturity based on a covenant love (1 Samuel 23:18) and a compassionate commitment (Philippians 2:20-21).

12. You can become a **partner of intentional encouragement** (P.I.E.) through the practical application of the above in your daily life. By reaching out to a friend, you can help create an ongoing mentoring system.

CHAPTER TWO
The Majesty of Encouragement: Living with Incredible Power

Priscilla and Aquila were a couple who revealed the power and majesty of God in their lives. They were transformed by the spirit of God and were motivated by His love to intentionally encourage others. They had a marriage of deep commitment and mutual respect. They were a husband and wife team dedicated to honoring God and equipping others to serve Him.

Apollos was one person whom they encouraged in living to his maximum God-given potential. Desiring to help him become more effective in his teaching, *"they invited him to their home and explained to him the way of God more adequately"* (Acts 18:26). The lives of Priscilla and Aquila revealed the majesty of God in motion.

Majesty is usually associated with kings, queens, and leaders who make great efforts to display their power and glory. However, their power is acquired, temporary, and external. It is a superficial display that quickly disappears with changing circumstances, death, and the passing of time. Real majesty, on the other hand, is connected with God. In contrast with human majesty, it is innate, lasting, eternal, and internal.

One dictionary definition of majesty is "exalted dignity, stateliness, or grandeur [or] sovereign authority."ᵛ This description is perfectly true of God, for He is the ultimate authority who is not limited or bounded by time. The Bible adds to this definition of **majesty** as "the greatness" and the "magnificence" of God.ᵛⁱ The Greek word for majesty is *megaliotes*. The first part of this word is 'mega,' from which we get our English word *mega,* as in a **great** project. God not only has greatness—He *is* **greatness**. God is not only majestic—He **is** majesty (Hebrews 1:3). God always acts out of what and who He is by nature. One of Jesus' first disciples, Peter, wrote:

> We were not making up clever stories when we told you about the power of our Lord Jesus Christ and his coming again. We have seen his majestic splendor with our own eyes. (2 Peter 1:16, NLT)

MAJESTY IN RELATIONSHIPS

The majesty of God is fully revealed in and through Jesus, who is Emmanuel, God with us (Matthew 1:23). The awesome greatness of God is never static, but always dynamic in nature. This greatness, confirmed by Peter in the quotation above, is expressed by the life of Jesus who is God the Son. He became man in order to offer eternal life to all who would choose to trust in Him by faith (John 1:12,14). It is seen in the relationships of Jesus. At the baptism of Jesus, the Father affirmed, the Holy Spirit empowered, and Jesus submitted. Jesus submitted to God's call for Him to accomplish His work as Savior for all who receive Him. This is a beautiful picture of God—Father, Son, and Holy Spirit—in intimate and harmonious relationship. This is majesty in motion—majesty in dynamic relationship!

When He was baptized by John, Jesus was encouraged by God the Father so that He could encourage us as human beings (Matthew 3:17). Jesus constantly practiced encouragement—offering life, and coming alongside of and strengthening the hearts of those who receive Him by faith. He walked intimately with the Father (John 10:30). Out of that intimacy, and by the leading of the Father through the Holy Spirit, Jesus reached out with sensitivity, love, and grace to others in need. Consider the woman who was avoided, gossiped about, struggling and lonely. As a Samaritan woman with a messed-up personal life, she was avoided by the Jews and despised by her community. But the perfect encourager—Jesus Himself—reaches out in love and sensitive, caring grace to understand, connect with, and call this person into the loving, healing embrace of the God who saves, heals, and transforms (John 4:25-26).

Real, authentic encouragement—the attitude and heart that reflects the greatness of God through the warm, caring filter of God's grace—is meant to be constantly active in the lives of every follower of Jesus. As God the Father sent Jesus on a life mission, so Jesus sends us to make passionate disciples whose personal lives display God's *majesty in motion!* Majesty speaks of the awe-inspiring grandeur of God. Encouragement is crucial, because it empowers us to act and allow God to display His greatness and tell His redemptive story through each of our unique personalities, which are

19

designed for that purpose! Let God's grace or generosity flow through you (1 Peter 4:10).

Choosing to communicate the majesty or greatness of God through personal relationships requires:

- putting others first.
- understanding God's heart for them.
- choosing to see them through the eyes of Jesus.
- getting closer so as to understand them.
- showing love without conditions.
- gently influencing them towards God.
- providing space and a necessary **affirming** environment for them to become the persons God intends.
- choosing to pay the price necessary for their sake and for God's glory.

MAJESTY IN LIVING (LIFESTYLE)

It is an incredible thing that God has invited us to reveal His majesty to the world by living a life of intentional encouragement. It means choosing to allow Jesus to live His divine life through you. It is deciding to live in community by imitating Jesus in thought, word, and action (Philippians 2:1-11). This way of living is called holiness.

Holiness is not a static mindset or position. It is a process of growing deeper into God, experiencing union with His heart, and expressing His character in creative and surprising ways to others you meet in daily life. God is a dynamic, creative, and active God who acts differently in various situations even while remaining the same in character, essence, and heart. We are each designed to be creative in our approach to life and people. Holiness is not a rigid system of do's and don'ts. Irwin McManus states the following:

> We have put so much emphasis on avoiding evil that we have become virtually blind to the endless opportunities for doing good. We have defined holiness through what we separate ourselves from than what we give ourselves to. I'm convinced that the great tragedy is not the sins we commit but the life we fail to live.[vii]

Ron is a guy who is learning to live a holy life and communicate the majesty of God in effective but gentle ways. He had been going back his life following his passion for the great outdoors. Ron made a living by leading wilderness camping and canoe trips. Later, he married and fathered children. Then, suddenly one day, he met tragedy while on a routine drive in his city. A man in a pick-up truck attempted to read a map while driving toward a stop sign at an intersection. He never stopped, crashing right into Ron's vehicle. Ron was severely injured.

But Ron did not give up. Through the process of rehabilitation, he determined to recover while relying on the compassion of God. During this time, his wife left him and Ron was on his own. In response, Ron did not grow bitter, but better. He did not dwell on *what if,* but on what he could now become by the grace of God. Today, Ron lives alone, but is actively involved as a chef in our city, as member of our church, and as a friend to all who take the time to know him. Ron is a vivid example of one human being who chooses to be an intentional encourager and demonstrate the majesty of God through holy living.

Practical Steps for Individuals and Small Groups

1. There are several references to Priscilla and Aquila in the New Testament. Find the references and determine why God used these two people so effectively.

2. Priscilla and Aquila obviously worked well as a couple. How can you make the partnership with your spouse (if you are married) work just as well?

3. How is majesty defined in this chapter? How did Jesus model the majesty of God the Father? What can you do to imitate Jesus and demonstrate the majesty of God in all of your relationships, starting in your marriage and family?

4. Review the eight ways in this chapter in which you can communicate or demonstrate the majesty of God to others. Begin a plan to develop these more deeply in your own life with inspiration and accountability from a partner of intentional encouragement (P.I.E.), or with feedback and support from your small group.

5. What does a lifestyle of **majestic living** look like? Review the quotation from Erwin McManus and examine your life to see how you measure up at this moment.

CHAPTER THREE
The Mission of Encouragement

EXTRAORDINARY LIVING

Real encouragement starts with character—specifically the character of God. Personal actions flow out of what you are becoming as a person. God says: *"You must be holy because I, the Lord your God, am holy"* (Leviticus 19:2, NLT). The word 'holy' has the meanings of being separate, bright, pure, and whole. It implies that God is separate from ordinary sinful human living. He is separate in that He exists and lives on a higher level. God is not common but uncommon. He is not ordinary but extra-ordinary. Jesus confirms this when He explains that God is not mere flesh and blood, but He is Spirit (John 4:24). God is outside of time and without limits, except those limits determined by His own nature. He is all-powerful and all-wise, living in perfect harmony with Jesus, the Son, and the Holy Spirit. The only way to enter the holy presence of God is by faith in Jesus, the Son (a combination of perfect God and perfect man), who bridged the gap between us sinful human beings and the Holy God (see Appendix A).

Evidence that God lives on a radically different level than us is seen in a story involving the disciple Peter, who had been out all night on the Sea of Galilee attempting to catch fish. Peter and the other fishermen totally failed—they did not catch even one fish! The next day, Jesus told Peter to *"go out where it is deeper and let down your nets, and you will catch many fish"* (Luke 5:4, NLT). Peter started to complain, but then realized that he should obey Jesus. He says, *"But if you say so, I'll let the nets down again"* (Luke 5:5, NLT).

When he did as Jesus commanded, the fishing nets suddenly became so full of fish that they began to tear and break apart. The awareness of this great miracle (How did Jesus know where the fish were located?) brought a sense of awe in Peter's heart! Realizing the sinfulness of his own heart in the presence of Jesus, Peter asked Jesus to leave him. Peter realized that his own sinfulness made him unworthy to be in the presence of Jesus, the Son of God. He realized that Jesus was no ordinary man. He was the Son of the living God, whose extraordinary divine essence enabled Him to perform extraordinary miracles. Jesus not only created all things, but as God the Son, He knows all things (John 1:3). Jesus lives on a higher level.

Peter was in the process of learning that he was also called to join his Savior, Jesus, on this higher level of being and living. God calls you also to be holy as He is holy (Leviticus 19:2). Jesus said He had come so that we "may have life and have it to the full" (John 10:10). The word 'full' can be translated as *abundant* or *extraordinary*. As one of God's encouragers, you are called to be and to live on a higher level of living—to develop the character that reflects the unique and extraordinary heart and character of God. When explaining that God is Spirit, Jesus says that *"those who worship him must worship in spirit and in truth"* (John 4:24, NLT). As human beings, we tend to live only on the physical level. There is far more to life than what we can see. Indeed, the spiritual level is the core of our being—eternal and lasting (2 Corinthians 4:18). This spiritual higher dimension gives meaning to our physical living.

The towering cliff seemed almost vertical to the beach and ocean shoreline below. As a boy growing up on a large island beside the ocean, I would often look upon the top of that cliff and wonder about climbing up to see the awesome view it offered at the top. In recent years, the government built a hiking path that twisted back and forth until it reached the summit. On a return trip back home, I determined to climb to that higher level. With a great burst of energy, I began to hike. Nearing the summit, my breathing grew more rapid and my heart began to pound. My pounding heart was as much or more due to my increasing excitement than the physical effort.

As I neared the summit, I could see glimpses of the ocean far below. Arriving there, I took in a vista so beautiful and moving that I burst out singing the words:

> O God, you are my God, I will ever praise
> you. I will praise you in the morning; I'll
> praise you all day long...

Far below, the wave tops glistened like gold in the sunlight. The seabirds majestically rode the air currents above the bay below. I could see three arms of the ocean on three sides. The woods smelled wonderful. It was an incredible buffet of sight, sound, and smell which reminded me that I could now see a

*whole different view because I had dared to move up to a
higher level!*

To reflect the heart of God to others, I need to *live with God
on His level.* I can do this by inviting Jesus, the Son of God, to
come into my life, forgive all my sins, transform my heart and
mind, and direct my life. As a Christian, I become a member
of God's new family of faith in Jesus, making me a citizen of
Heaven. As a citizen of Heaven who still lives in this present
world, I am called to act as a representative of God to others.
"We are citizens of heaven, where the Lord Jesus Christ lives"
(Philippians 3:20, NLT). *"Therefore, we are Christ's ambassadors, and God is using us to speak to [you]"* (2 Corinthians
5:20, NLT).

LASER LIGHT

The word holy, in reference to God, means more than extraordinary living. It means to be 'light' or 'bright.' God is
light (1 John 1:5). God is also called the Father of lights
(James 1:17). The Bible defines light as that which exposes,
reveals, or uncovers. Light dispels darkness in a physical or
moral sense. Darkness is often symbolic of sin or evil. God's
kingdom, or sphere of rule, is full of light. When you turn
from selfishness and self-dependence to trust completely in
Jesus as your Savior by faith, you are 'adopted' into God's
eternal family and you begin a new life of shining forth the
light of God to others. God calls you out of darkness into the
spiritual light of Jesus (1 Peter 2:9).

The majesty of the brilliant light of God is meant to be
dwelling in you. It is God's intention that you become a
showcase for His light. The light of God is like a laser. The

27

light of a laser is intensely focused, so concentrated that it exposes, cuts, and heals when used intentionally for a specific purpose. God's encourager yields himself to Jesus, allowing Jesus to live out His life through the person's unique personality. Jesus declared that He is *"the light of the world"* (John 8:12). But it is also equally true that each follower of Jesus is also a *"light of the world"* (Matthew 5:14). How is this possible? It is possible because Jesus, who is the light, shines His awesome, divine light through your life and personality! Let Jesus be *the number one priority and authority in you* and you can be a 'laser light'—becoming a gentle, exposing, revealing, and healing influence in the life of your friend or coworker. Think of how that will change the life of a family, the life of a worker, and the long-term health of a business that treats customers and employees as valuable. The potential of a generative ripple effect is enormous!

Employees at the store of a major retailer actually enjoyed going to work. I chose to work part-time for four months at this store because it would give me ample opportunity to interact a lot with both employees and customers. As an intentional encourager, my approach was to pray continuously for employees with whom I worked directly. It was not long before certain employees approached me to share a need, to ask about my faith, or even to ask for prayer. After a while, I noticed that working became enjoyable despite the low pay and stressful circumstances. My prayer was also that God would shine through my attitude, words, and work in such a way that customers would be best served and that the retailer would benefit. It was a win-win situation! Some customers did respond by expressing their appreciation to my employer.

28

When I communicated my intention to leave, a store manager urged me to stay, but a fellow employee said, "He's moving on to a higher calling." I was simply one ordinary person who wanted to be an intentional encourager for God. God chose to act as a laser light into the lives of some persons with whom I worked.

PURE AND POTENT

The word holy has a third component: *purity.* To say that God is holy is to say that God is absolutely pure. This means that God is unmixed with any sin—there are no impurities in Him. As sinful human beings, we are impure, a state that can only be changed by inviting the pure Jesus to live in us. To be pure is to have a heart that is pure, a heart that reflects the heart of Jesus Christ (1 John 3:3).

A pure heart has a potent impact. When baking, a flavor that is concentrated and pure has a potent effect that impacts an entire batch of dough. Pure vanilla will give the product an unmistakable flavor. Indeed, a vanilla cake will spread its fragrance throughout the house.

In the same way, Jesus teaches that if you seek to spend time and effort listening, seeking, worshipping, trusting, and feeding on God through His written word, the Bible, you will develop a pure mind and spirit that reflects God and allows God to work in an amazingly pure and powerful way through you to others around you! Purity is not weakness, but greatness in the most effective way possible—impacting others with godly character! So, choose pure thinking and pure living, for those who do, will truly see God (Matthew 5:8). Jesus puts it this way:

> You are the salt of the earth. But what
> good is salt if it has lost its flavor? Can you
> make it useful again? It will be thrown out
> and trampled underfoot as worthless.
> (Matthew 5:13, NLT)

Real lasting encouragement requires far more than the right mood, feeling, or even the right attitude. It requires the right character. Someone once said:

> A choice made often enough becomes a
> habit. A habit builds a character. A charac-
> ter determines a destiny.

This destiny might be the ultimate destiny of the one you love the most. Your mission of encouragement is to allow God to work through you so that He can transform the present and guarantee the future of those who receive and embrace Him with open arms of unleashed faith and unconditional commitment. God eagerly searches for those who seek to live a life of unhesitating intimacy with Him and who possess a willingness to serve Him and represent Him clearly in a world of human beings focused inwardly on themselves.

> The eyes of the Lord search the whole
> earth in order to strengthen those whose
> hearts are fully committed to him. (2
> Chronicles 16:9, NLT)

Practical Steps for Individuals and Small Groups

1. Becoming holy and living a holy life is essential to becoming an intentional encourager. How is **holy** described in Chapter 3?

2. What lesson did Peter learn about holiness? Are *you* willing to pay the necessary price to purify your heart and live on a higher level as God requires?

3. If you are a Christian, your citizenship is already established in heaven, even though you are living now on earth. Read Philippians 3:17-21. How should you live as a heavenly citizen within the context of ordinary earthly living?

4. Review the four major components of **holy** as seen in Chapter 3. Which one is most needed now in your life? What can you do to ensure that you are growing to be more laser-focused, or pure and potent?

5. Remember that you must first experience God's majesty and encouragement in your own life *before* you can inspire someone else to become an intentional encourager for God.

CHAPTER FOUR
What Has Love Got to Do with It?

Echoing the words of an old rock song, you might wonder, "What does love got to do with it?" Real lasting encouragement can never be expressed to another without communicating it in love. Western popular culture views 'love' as a physical attraction to or a sexual desire for someone. Many people talk about 'making love.' The phrase 'I love you' in Western culture often means that I love your body, your appearance, your money, your connections, or at least something that I can see. It is often very superficial—usually the stuff of talk shows or nightly entertainment.

But the love which fuels a mindset, attitude, and life of encouragement permeates far deeper and produces results that last much longer than the 'love' of popular culture. Human love is obviously mixed in motive, sporadic in performance, and variable in its results. If it depends on me alone, my love for you will be influenced by the benefits I receive in return. That is true whether it is showing love to my family or to a stranger. In each case, I want to feel good about it and even have others think I am a loving person.

If I really want to be an intentional encourager who inspires others forward and strengthens their heart for lasting accomplishments, I need a love that reaches beyond myself. Because this love must be animate and personal, it is necessary that this love flow from the only One who is beyond ordinary humans like you and me. This requires the love of God. If my dependence is on God, I can love you not only for who you are, but for who you can become. Like the mistake-prone, impulsive disciple Peter, I am also a recipient of God's love, which gives me the opportunity to grow into my ultimate purpose and destiny.

The majesty or the greatness of God's love is perfectly balanced. It is both an intentional act that transforms and an emotion that inspires. Love—real love—is not primarily a feeling, but an action. The Hebrew term *chesed* refers to the covenant love of God. As in a marriage, covenant love is an intentional act of choosing to give to another the very best that you have. In reference to God, it means His willingness to bless all who are obedient to Him by faith. It is done not because of our qualifications, but because God chooses to give His very best to us through His Son, Jesus. The ultimate act of His love was expressed when He gave His life on a cross so that each one who receives Jesus into their hearts as Savior and director can receive life, now and forever! *Chesed* love is unconditional—God did not wait for your response to love you. It is sacrificial—God even sacrificed His Son for you on the cross. It is without hesitation—God did not and does not hesitate to come to your rescue. It is sensitive and caring—by coming to us on our human level, the infinite God of creation intentionally identifies with us in our every need, and desires to help others through you.

The Hebrew meaning of *chesed* love is completely fulfilled in the life, death, and resurrection of Christ—described in the Greek term *agape*. *Agape* is the word used to describe both Christ's love for us and our love for others. We can only love other Christians by allowing His love to minister through us to them (Ephesians 5:1-2). *Agape's* essential meaning, in the biblical context, is the intent of the heart to act in a sacrificial, unconditional, proactive spirit to meet the needs of another. This is exactly what the Lord Jesus has done and will do for all who are willing to invite him into their hearts by faith. It is this combination of the intentional action of *chesed* and *agape* love, infused by the Christ-like caring emotion of *aheb* love, that can transform you into one of God's inspiring intentional encouragers! *Aheb* love is described below.

Starting with His covenant with Abraham, and concluding with His new covenant based on the person and work of Jesus, God has committed Himself forever to all who come to trust in His Son by faith. Covenant love means that God's love never fails. Even when a dedicated follower of Jesus sins or stumbles or goes astray in any way, God never ceases to love that person. Israel's famous king David abused his position of authority. He lusted for the wife of another man, Uriah, and ordered her to be brought to his palace. David compounded his sin with Bathsheba by trying to cover up his sin for many months. After finding out that Bathsheba was pregnant, he sought to place the blame on Uriah, her husband. When that did not work, he ordered his loyal soldier Uriah to be placed on the frontlines of battle so that he would be killed. After being confronted by God's prophet, Nathan, David repents and tearfully confesses his sin to God: *"Have mercy on me, O God, because of your unfailing love"* (Psalm 51:1, NLT).

David had no excuse. The only basis on which he could come to God with any hope was due to the *chesed* love of God, which was based not on David's character or actions, but on the pure character of God. Covenant love is based on God's unchanging love. But contractual love is subject to the whims and desires of the giver and recipient of love. A contract can be changed if one of the partners wants more benefit for himself. However, the covenant love of God, when expressed through your personality, always seeks the best for the person in need. You will not betray or desert a person in need, but faithfully support him or her. Why? Because God influences and motivates you as a true intentional encourager. *human love, being a friend, to like*

Such commitment to choice is balanced by emotion in the heart of God. The Hebrew word *aheb* means to feel for another person. The act of intentionally choosing the best for us in God's mind, is balanced with the expression of delight for us as He acts. This word refers to God's command for the people of Israel to love (or *delight to help)* the foreigner, stranger, or newcomer among them (Leviticus 19:34). With this word, God is saying, "Since I rejoice and delight in giving my best to you, I want you to rejoice in helping, encouraging others with the same needs." God told them to love them as they would love themselves or act as if you were in their shoes. The people of Israel could encourage others by loving them because God first loved them and met their every need.

> Do not exploit the foreigners who live in your land. They should be treated like everyone else, and you must love them as

you love yourself. Remember that you were once foreigners in the land of Egypt. I, the Lord, am your God. (Leviticus 19:33-34, NLT).

Practical Steps for
Individuals and Small Groups

1. Intentional encouragement is only possible with love. But this requires a growing understanding and intimate experience of the real thing. What instantly comes to your mind when you see or hear the word 'love'?

2. The Hebrew word *chesed* refers to a love that is perfectly realized in God. Review Chapter 4 and list specific qualities of this love. Since God calls you to reflect His love to others, what changes are needed in your life for *chesed* love to fully develop in you?

3. The statement "God's love is a balanced love" is presented in this chapter. What does it mean to **possess and express** a balanced love?

4. Balanced love is also covenant love. How does the word *covenant* define love, especially as it is expressed in the life of Jesus?

5. What are the meanings of the terms *chesed*, *agape*, and *aheb* regarding love as expressed in this chapter? All three together produce the genuine love that seeks to understand, connect with, inspire, and really help a discouraged person that you may know.

6. Examine your own life. What specific actions can you take to spark the growth of this threefold love required to make you an intentional encourager?

7.   Begin a plan of action with an appropriate partner of intentional encouragement (P.I.E.). This is best done within the larger context of a small care group to which you belong.

CHAPTER FIVE
The Lift of Encouragement

ACHIEVING LIFT IN A SNOWSTORM

A Northwest Airlines Boeing 757 circled and circled the skies above the Detroit area during a winter blizzard. When the plane ahead of us landed, we began our final descent into the airport. It was just the beginning of several hours of unexpected and unwanted drama—at least from my point of view. It was impossible to see the runway, or even the airport terminal, from my window view.

Once our plane landed safely, we taxied up to the terminal building and then filed into the building. I had another plane to catch to Minneapolis, but it was obvious that we were not leaving anytime soon. The agent announced that it would be a long wait, but my flight was still scheduled to take off in the snowstorm. After about a three-hour wait, my fellow passengers and I boarded a jumbo DC-10.

I got increasingly nervous and my hands began to sweat. No other planes seemed to be taking off as darkness fell and the blinding snow continued and the winds howled.

Sometimes, a little knowledge is a dangerous thing. I was no aviation expert, but as an aviation fan, I knew that deicing the wings of the plane and its lift surfaces was crucial to our getting off the ground. As we waited in the plane, I could see ice and snow building up on the wings. I remembered the crash of an Air Florida plane in Washington, D.C. due to ice build-up on the wings and I was not ready to die yet! Seeing no action on this as I looked out the window, I stopped the first flight attendant that I saw. About two minutes later, the pilot announced that deicing was being done and that he would never fly without it.

After what seemed like an eternity, our plane began its roll down the runway while the snow continued to fall. I kept praying, Lord, please get us up to cruising altitude!

The plane made it off the ground. As it gained altitude, the plane suddenly made a jerking motion as if it was stalling, but soon continued up to its planned cruising altitude. Finally, we made it to Minneapolis and clear, calm weather!

Ah! The power of **lift**! The Bible speaks frequently of the reason Jesus came to earth—to lift all who receive Him to a higher level (John 10:10, Joshua 7:13,15, Matthew 9:35-39). Unless you are living on a higher spiritual level through faith in Jesus, you cannot lift someone else. You can only lift and inspire others to a higher level of living as you experience it yourself.

When there is ice on the leading edges of the wings, a plane loses its ability to overcome the effects of the law of gravity. In your life, the 'ice' is known as sin. Sin in our human lives acts like ice, robbing us of our ability to live on a higher spiritual level in Jesus. When that happens, you lose the power to lift someone else. Sin is any attitude, thought, or act that causes you to reject, resist, or ignore the revealed will and word of God given to us in the Bible.

THE POWER OF ONE

It takes only one person to crash or lift a plane. It takes only one spouse to destroy a marriage. By your spirit or attitude, you can weaken or lift your family, undermine or strengthen your workplace. Think of inspirational athletes such as Tom Brady in football, or Wayne Gretzky in hockey, who inspired their teams by their attitude and example. These men would not let their teams fail.

The Bible tells the story of one person who literally saved the lives of thousands. His name was Phinehas. He deeply trusted God and he loved his fellow citizens. A crisis quickly developed as a plague spread though the population. As a nation, Israel was living in flagrant sin, despising God's word and despising His name. In response, God began to judge His people with the plague.

However, Phinehas boldly approached God to plead for the deliverances of His people. The Bible describes the scene:

> They provoked the Lord to anger by their wicked deeds, and a plague broke out among them. But Phinehas stood up and intervened, and the plague was checked. (Psalm 106:29-30)

Nu 25.1-13

Consider the power of one person. Consider Phinehas. If you are willing to live in obedience to God and honor Him in all your ways, your prayers can touch the heart of God, just like those of Phinehas.

Think of the power of your own life and example. Dedicate your life to honoring God and helping anyone you meet to develop to their fullest potential. The result will be extraordinary influence in the greatest possible way, from the barber shop to the coffee shop. Like an eagle, you can develop a wider perspective instead of a narrow vision. When you are willing to soar with God in your spiritual life, you will be able to see needs of the wider world and needs of the whole person, because you will see others as God sees them. This is the perspective of Jesus.

An intentional encourager sees a person for whom he or she can become. If I want to become such an encourager, I will seek to treat you as if you are more valuable than I am. This means that I want to help you experience God's very best. In such a mindset, there is no room for selfishness, jealousy, or envy. It is not that you are more valuable than the other person, but that you treat him or her as if they were. As an intentional encourager, you are more secure in who you are because you belong to God and serve Him with an unchanging purpose. The consequence is a person who delights to lift up all those she meets. It is being others-centered.

> Do nothing out of selfish ambition or vain conceit, but in humility consider others better than yourselves. Each of you should look not only to your own interests, but also to the interests of others. Your attitude should be the same as that of Christ Jesus. (Philippians 2:3-5).

> Treat a man as he appears to be and you make him worse. But treat a man as if he already were what he potentially could

42

be, and you make him what he should be.[viii]

In your home, group of friends, or workplace, you can build a context of caring for someone whenever they need it. The intention is then to encourage that person to 'be there' for someone else just in time. Some automakers avoid costly inventories and maintain an efficient flow of vehicles by arranging for auto parts to arrive just in time for the need on the assembly line. By developing a sensitive mindset, a constant awareness of others in need, and a caring compassionate heart, you can change a family, a community, and even deeply impact the world by offering loving help to a friend, stranger, or a critic 'just in time.'

STARTING THOUGHTS?

IDENTIFY & PRACTICE
ENCOURAGING SIGNALS

Practical Steps for Individuals and Small Groups

1. Achieving lift is crucial to getting anywhere in an airplane or making forward progress in a sailboat. You need to make sure that the plane's wings have clean leading edges and that your boat's sail has its sail trimmed at the proper angle to the wind. In this chapter, Jesus is quoted as saying that He came to lift you to a higher level of living. Using the above analogies, examine the 'wings' or 'sails' in your life. Is there any sin, unforgiveness, pride, selfishness, or lack of self-control that prevents the 'wind' of God from lifting you?

2. Consider the brief story of Phinehas as described in Psalm 106:29-31. What can you do regarding your own relationship with God to be more effective in your prayers for others?

3. Carefully read through Philippians 2. What specific qualities of Jesus do you need to develop more in your life?

4. Review the quotation from Goethe. How you treat someone may have enormous implications for what they will become. How are you treating persons close to you in:
   - Your family.
   - Your group or team.
   - Your workplace.

- Your community organization.
- Your neighborhood.

5. List specific names in the above categories and begin a plan for treating them as God (and you, hopefully) want them to become.

CHAPTER SIX
The Friendship Store

Wal-Mart announced that their store in our neighborhood would now be open 24 hours a day. Their intention is to be available to their loyal customers whenever the need arises. Wow—24-hour shopping!

Do I need this? I don't need 24-hour shopping, but I do need the **availability** of a friend, at any time, at all times. It is not that I want that friend to be with me at all times, but it is crucial for me to know that I can count on a true friend when I need help. Therefore, I want my family, my work team, and my church to act as a 24-hour Friendship Store. In my friendship store, I want my family, group, or church to act as God's *listening* ear, *seeing* eye, *caring* heart, and *helping* hands. However, this does not mean that you should allow someone to consume all of your time, energy, and attention. Being a friend to that kind of person means to be firm and to help them set personal boundaries.

The Bible says that *"a friend is always loyal, and a brother is born to help in time of need"* (Proverbs 17:17, NLT). Such a friend does not accept immoral or wrong behavior, but cares enough to confront in love and provide a context to inspire that person to choose change that leads to transformation in the long-term. My home or church ought to be the first place where such a needy person can not only survive, but learn to live in honor of God and the good of others. Are you willing to be a true friend, willing to be there for someone in time of need? *"There are 'friends' who destroy each other, but a real friend sticks closer than a brother"* (Proverbs 18:24, NLT).

You may find it difficult to be that kind of friend. You may find it hard to get close to others in need because you have experienced some past abuse or hurt that makes you wary of others. Others may see this and not want to act as a friend to you. The answer is found in choosing to bring yourself close to God, who knows you far more deeply than you know yourself. And yet, He loves you with an everlasting, unconditional love. Ask God to take complete direction and ownership of your life. It may take considerable time. Start today! Ask Him to give you a heart of love for that person who seems unlovable to you.

In your marriage, and in other relationships, the closer you grow towards Jesus as owner and director of your heart, the closer you will get to your spouse or the other person. Because of His atoning death and resurrection, Jesus has not only *"broken down the wall of hostility"* (Ephesians 2:14, NLT), but continues to break down walls with you, between you and God, and between you and others when you allow Him to live His life through you. Great news! God is in the business of not only restoring you, but restoring relationships for you and through you in your family, church, and community.

In the words of Richard Exley:

A true friend is one who hears and understands when you share your deepest feelings. He supports you when you are struggling. He corrects you gently and with love when you err, and he forgives you when you fail. A true friend prods you to personal growth, stretches you to full potential. And, most amazing of all, he celebrates your successes as if they were his very own.[ix]

Are you willing to be this kind of a friend? Are you willing to live in such a way as to lift up others, contribute to their success, and rejoice in their triumph? This is always true of she or he who chooses to transform others through intentional encouragement.

A ROYAL EXAMPLE

He was anointed to be the leader of his nation. There was an obstacle in the way, though: the position was not yet open. Meanwhile, he continued to worship God, serve his country, and fulfill his family role by taking care of sheep in the fields. His name was David. David soon became a hero to his fellow citizens because of his strong faith in God and his military success against the Philistines, the enemy of his native Israel. After courageously facing and killing Goliath, David was soon praised by the crowds. The present king Saul soon turned from friend to foe as his jealousy of David consumed his remaining years of rule. David was hounded and relentlessly pursued so much that one day he reached the proverbial end of his rope. This one day was one of the lowest, most depressing times of his life. He felt physically, emotionally, and even spiritually ex-

48

hausted. What was David to do? If ever he was in need of a supporting friend, it was now.

Amazingly, the rescue came in the form of the son of David's sworn enemy! The Bible describes it in these words:

> And Saul's son Jonathan went to David at Horesh and helped him find strength in God. (1 Samuel 23:16)

Jonathan knew that he had risked his own life to help David. If he was caught, Jonathan would likely have paid the ultimate price by losing his own life. Jonathan intentionally chose to encourage David by restoring his faith and joy in God. To strengthen David's hand was to help restore David's spiritual, emotional, mental, and physical resources to keep on living. In this context, *intentional encouragement* is **restoring David's will to live!**

Imagine yourself coming alongside a friend and restoring his or her will to live. Many of us are so busy with our plans and schedules that we fail to stop and seek to understand just a little of the struggle that a family member, co-worker, or neighbor is facing. Sometimes we are shocked when some person takes their own life. We thought that we knew him, but we really did not know him at all because we live our lives too superficially, never stopping to reflect on the real progress of another.

But this is the core of *intentional encouragement*—to intend to pay whatever price is necessary to understand, help, and inspire a spouse, child, neighbor, or friend. What made Jonathan's encouragement so effective? His encouragement was based on the covenant love of God (1 Samuel 23:18).

49

CONTRACT VERSUS COVENANT

A covenant is an agreement between two persons or parties based on commitment, trust, and transparency. Covenant finds its basis in God, who first made a covenant with Abraham (Genesis 12:1). When God initiates a covenant, He never fails to abide by it. God's love and grace is unfailing because God Himself never fails us. When God declares His love for you, it is absolutely reliable. You can count on God even though He cannot always count on you or me. We can trust that God will always forgive and love us through his new covenant in Jesus Christ (Ephesians 4:32). If you commit yourself fully and unconditionally to God, He can love and lift another person through you. Based on God's unfailing love, you can be that intentionally encouraging friend who is **always there in time of need**.

What a contrast with contract love! Contracts between individuals and parties are made to be broken. Many sign contracts, but then quickly seek to change them or break them when they no longer suit their interests. Contracts can be signed based on mutual greed, but genuine covenants are based on mutual care. Jonathan's covenant with David was based on his real love and care for David and not so much on himself. He reflected the heart of God in that he was others-centered.

AN OLYMPIC EFFORT

During the 1992 Olympics, a British runner named Derek Redmond was in the middle of a race when he suddenly stumbled and fell. He had torn a ligament and quickly discovered that his hopes for a medal were lost. Desperately attempting to run, he struggled and soon slowed to a crawl. Meanwhile, fel-

low competitors ran past him toward the finish line. While he struggled to move forward, a man ran out of the spectator stands, past startled guards, and onto the racing track.

This man lowered himself toward the ground, put his shoulder under Derek's arm and lifted Derek—assisting him in his excruciatingly painful walk toward the finish line. Who was that man? It was none other than Derek's father!

Derek's father acted as an **intentional encourager** that day. He put himself in Derek's situation. He 'felt' the pain of Derek in his own heart. He wanted the best for Derek and was willing to pay a price of his own for another person in need—in this case, his own son. He was willing to lower himself to the level of a person in need so that he could lift him up to a higher level and enable him to reach the finish line. Each of us has the opportunity to do this for persons who live near us or work with us.

Derek's dad is an example of a real 24-hour friend. He made himself available to help his son at any time of need. Such friends need not always come from the same biological family. They ought to come from members of your church, club, team, or neighborhood. Such 24-hour friends treat a person in genuine need as if they were a brother, sister, or parent. This attitude reflects genuine love perfectly, as revealed through the character of Jesus.

Practical Steps for Individuals and Small Groups

1. A true **friend** is someone who really cares enough to encourage you, regardless of the circumstances. She or he is not one who likes you in good times and abandons or betrays you to suit their desires—such a person is a fair-weather friend who 'cares' about you only for their selfish purposes. (In the Bible, read Psalm 41:9 and Psalm 55:12-14 to prepare you for those who want to 'encourage' only for themselves and not for you). What does the word 'friend' mean to you?

2. Carefully read and study the following bible references. How does God define a true friend? How can you develop such characteristics and behavior in your life to make anyone else feel at home in your presence?
    *   Proverbs 17:17 and 27:6
    *   Ecclesiastes 4:10
    *   Exodus 33:11
    *   John 15:14-15

3. Review and reflect on the **friendship store** analogy. Prayerfully choose others who can help you create this culture of friendship and availability for others who enter your home, group, church, or organiza-

tion. What actual step can you take to do this in a spiritual context?

4. Note Richard Exley's definition of a true friend. How does his description compare with your present life and relationships with those around you?

5. The true story of Jonathan's friendship with the future king David is an inspiring model for everyone. Review this material from 1 Samuel 23:16-18. Identify someone in your circles of influence who desperately needs another woman or man to come alongside them and help them to pull back from the brink of darkness. Are you willing to inconvenience yourself and **pay the necessary price** to help or get help for that person?

6. As you think about the story of the Olympian, ask yourself: Do I know someone who has broken through obstacles to **lift me up when I fell down?** Am I prepared to do the same for someone else by putting myself in their shoes?

7. Define **contract** love versus **covenant** love. See the description in the Jonathan-David friendship in this chapter. What does it take to possess and apply covenant love to someone else? (See Genesis 12:1-3 for a clue.)

PART TWO

THE FOUNDATION OF INTENTIONAL ENCOURAGEMENT

INTRODUCTION

Once you have discovered the incredible life of intentional encouragement, you will desire to live this life every day. But anything worthwhile has a price. What price are you willing to pay to be an intentional encourager? If you are willing to give yourself fully to honor God and become a constant encourager of everyone you meet, a rock solid foundation must be built into your life. This is not an 'instant,' static concept, but a foundational process of three key qualities that are necessary to keep the light of encouragement shining through you. These qualities are like the oil necessary in an old lamp to keep the wick shining bright. Your life will shine ever brighter as long as the fuel is continually supplied! There was an old song with the words, "Give me oil in my lamp, keep me burning." The three qualities providing the 'oil' or fuel needed for an encouraging life are joy, patience, and peace.

CHAPTER SEVEN
The Joy-Motivated Life

An intentional encourager is motivated by a heart filled with joy. Joy is more than a feeling or heightened emotional state. Joy is a rock solid confidence that Jesus Christ lives in me and that I rest by faith completely in Him. It arises out of a deepening, growing relationship with God. This relationship does not break in any circumstance, but fuels my passion for living, my love for others, and my confidence in seeing opportunity and purpose in every situation. The passionate and brilliant Hebrew man Saul (whose name was changed to Paul after his encounter with God), explained the awesome accomplishments of his own life as an intentional encourager in these words:

> I myself no longer live, but Christ lives in me. So I live my life in this earthly body by trusting in the Son of God, who loved me and gave himself for me. (Galatians 2:20, NLT)

Paul often talked about joy, even though he suffered much to serve God and minister to others. Joy may include suffering, sorrow, and challenges of many kinds, but it is the mark of an intentional encourager whose trust rests in God who is always in control of all things. If I am filled with the joy of Jesus, I will be motivated to break out of my comfort zone to connect with, understand, and inspire another person to find strength in God.

When you are truly connected with God in a faith relationship marked by obedience, joy fills your heart. Because of the active presence of God in you, your life becomes an overflow! The Hebrew root word for overflow is not a verb, but a noun. Out of your intimate relationship with God, you can **overflow!** Those who live in and out of the presence of God will *"still yield fruit in old age; they shall be full of sap and very green"* (Psalm 92:14, NASB). The picture of your life then emerges as a tree that gives forth its life giving juice when you touch it.

When transferred into a human context, this means that all those who come in contact with you during the course of a day will be touched by the joyful overflow of your heart! The Hebrew word for 'full of sap' is *fat*, meaning the state of bursting, ready to burst, or overflow. When joy overflows in your heart, you are ready to live life as a real intentional encouragement to others. This life is not lived in isolation, but as a passionate member of God's family—all those who are willing to trust in Jesus as their personal Savior, director, and God. *"We are called to draw each other forward on the healing path through courage giving care. We know the word as encouragement...the drawing forth of another's courage, strength, resolve and passion..."** Imagine joy increasing, enlarging like a fire inside of you. You cannot hide it or keep it!

The air was cold and wet. The lower slopes leading to the mountains were rugged and large enough in scale to be intimidating. As I hiked with three other persons along the path leading to the caves and hot springs on the slopes of Sulfur Mountain in Banff National Park, God's creation was breathtaking. I was overwhelmed and awed with God as Creator.

When we arrived at the caves and approached the hot springs bubbling up from deep in the earth, the smell of sulfur became strong enough to block the smell of anything else. Now I knew why they called it Sulfur Mountain! I poked my finger into a bubbling stream. Despite the cold air, the emerging spring water was warm enough for a hot bath, but I was not about to try that! Columns of searing steam rose continuously into the air.

The hot springs of Banff remind me of the effects of joy in a person's life. It rises up, emerging as an overflow out of a heart filled with joy! The Hebrew prophet Jeremiah spoke of the effects of God's word like a fire within him.

> His word is in my heart like a fire, a fire shut up in my bones. I am weary of holding it in; indeed I cannot. (Jeremiah 20:9).

Joy is like that—an emerging confidence in God as Creator, Savior, and Shepherd that cannot be denied. Another way of understanding the joy-filled and joy-motivated life is to imagine the domino effect that you can have on the people who are closest to you.

One day, I entered a recreation complex and watched as a fountain continuously supplied water to a series of buckets attached to a pole. Each bucket was positioned at different heights on the pole. The fountain filled the first bucket, near the top, with water. As it filled up, the pressure of the water caused the bucket to tip over, spilling its contents into the next bucket below. As this one also filled up, the second bucket then tipped over and gave its water to the next bucket, until the water emptied into the waiting pool. This is an accurate illustration of what happens in me when the joy of Jesus fills my heart. His continuous joy in me moves my heart to 'fill' someone else with the love and grace of Jesus.

Jesus reminded His first disciples with these words as He sent them out into communities around them: *"Freely you have received, freely give"* (Matthew 10:8). As you deepen your spiritual roots in God, the more He will pour the waters of an enriching life into you so that you can give away this same life to others. It is never God's intention that we live like the Dead Sea—receiving water in, but giving nothing out. But like the Sea of Galilee, we are called to receive God's blessings and give away these blessings at the same time. Receive and give—that is the sign of a joy-motivated life! It is also the sign that you fully receive the forgiveness of God through Jesus Christ. A person who has fully received God's forgiveness will want to extend such forgiveness to others. Such a response to others will result in God's blessing returning to you.

> Give, and it will be given to you. A good
> measure, pressed down, shaken together
> and running over, will be poured into
> your lap. For with the measure you use, it
> will be measured to you. (Luke 6:38)

Speaking to growing disciples of Jesus, the Apostle Peter gave these God-inspired words:

60

> Though you have not seen him, you love
> him; and even though you do not see him
> now, you believe in him and are filled
> with an inexpressible and glorious joy. (1
> Peter 1:8).

Joy is a gracious confidence that arises out of the practice of an intimate fellowship with God (Psalm 16:11). It is God's intention to express the flavor of His person through your unique personality. One of the more exotic coffees marketed today is called 'Kopi Luwak.' The unique flavor of this coffee is the result of coffee beans passing through the digestive system of a large Asian cat. They are swallowed, but not crushed. People are willing to pay much more for this coffee than for a Starbuck's coffee. In a similar way, the joy of God is filtered through your personality or mine—flavored with your personality, but still clearly experienced as a gift from God. This can be majesty, the majesty of God in motion through you!

The foundation that ensures a more lasting encouragement requires not only joy in you, but an ability and willingness to take time for understanding your spouse, friend, or fellow worker. We live in a very impatient culture that bombards us with a million different distractions. The result is that we tend to live life on a very superficial level and ignore the real deeper needs of friends or strangers where we encounter them. That's why a joyful mindset must be reinforced with patience for every intentional encourager.

Practical Steps for Individuals and Small Groups

1. To consistently encourage others, you need to deeply experience encouragement by building a foundation of Christ-like qualities (Galatians 5:22-23). Three of these qualities—joy, peace, and patience—are the focus of the next three chapters. How is joy defined in this chapter?

2. Joy depends on the depth and health of your faith relationship with Jesus. Joy is not the absence of sadness or sorrow. Read again and memorize Galatians 2:20. To what degree does Christ Jesus direct your personal life? How can a Christian reconcile two vital truths: I live (am living), and yet Christ lives (is living) in me? Understanding this will increase your joy!

3. Joy is described as an **overflow** of God in your heart and mind. Read Psalm 84:4-7 and Psalm 92:12-14. From these references and this chapter, identify at least four specific, practical actions toward others you can take when you experience an overflow of God's joy.

4. In Psalm 23:5, King David wrote, *"My cup overflows."* In Hebrew, the text indicates that David has received the cup of saturation—saturated with God's presence. Joy is also the irrepressible motivation to

obey God's will and communicate His word. In this chapter, Jeremiah 20:9 and 1 Peter 1:8 are quoted. What steps can you take to increase your motivation to communicate the person and the word of Christ?

CHAPTER EIGHT
Patience: The Mark of Personal Security

To be an effective intentional encourager, revealing the **majesty** of God to others, you need patience and lots of it. To determine your level of patience, ask yourself questions such as:

- Am I always in a hurry?
- Do I often express frustration over little things?
- Am I easily upset with my children or my spouse at home?
- Am I easily impatient with others in my workplace?
- How would others describe my driving habits?
- Do I have a *meaningful* daily time with God?

- Am I too impatient to take time with God, to enter His presence, and really hear His voice?
- What kind of example am I being to my children and to others who are younger than I am?

In mentoring a young growing leader named Timothy, the brilliant and wise Apostle Paul wrote to him in the first century with these words: "Watch yourself *and* your teaching" (1 Timothy 4:16, paraphrased). In other words, watch your heart and your conduct in words and actions.

Someone once said that, since you cannot manage time, you must learn to manage yourself. Managing or disciplining yourself requires a lot of patience. The following scene is played out wherever a car culture exists. When you have a love for something or someone, you will find a way to take whatever time is necessary to draw out the best in the object of your love. If you are a lover of classic cars, you can easily imagine a scenario like this.

The old rusting, broken down, useless car was always in his sights whenever he returned to his yard. It reminded Robert of the junk, garbage, mess, and decaying vehicles and appliances that he saw scattered in ugly neglected parks and industrial sites around the region. He was a lover of cars—this one in particular.

Robert's frustration with that sight in his own yard gave rise to a dream. That dream enlarged to a vision of what that old Ford Mustang could become—restored to its former glory! His old Mustang could be reborn, able to operate according to its original purpose. It would require a huge amount of pa-

tience. But his love for this old car and a clear vision of its potential spurred him on. Launching into the restoration project, Robert began taking out the broken parts, removing and adding, filing and improving, cutting and polishing. Finally, the Mustang was ready to be revealed to family, friends, and visitors. The transformation of this car left its admirers in awe!

Now, think of individual persons whom you know who are broken, struggling, and who need someone with sufficient patience to take time for them. Rather than ignoring or avoiding them, they need you and me to make time to pray for them, making an effort to put ourselves in their shoes. God seeks persons like you to make a transforming difference in the life of such a person. Such persons can be restored to their original potential and become *"a new creation"* (2 Corinthians 5:17). Transforming people requires something that only God can give—huge amounts of patience. Such patience will be more readily available to you when you realize and give thanks for the incredible patience that God has displayed in your life!

Without the joy of Jesus filling your heart, you cannot encourage others to a deeper relationship of trust and faith in God. It is the indwelling presence of Jesus that will make others around you feel at home. It is this genuine authenticity—'feeling at home' with you—that enables them to passionately follow Christ within the context of an affirming group, team, or local church. But there are 'robbers' of encouragement that threaten to stop me or hinder me from having full access to God's very best—robbers such as impatience.

SCOUTING YOUR ENEMY—KEY TO WINNING

Since every person is impatient to some degree, how do we win over this enemy of impatience in our lives? We have to know the nature, characteristics, and strength of this enemy, as it prevents us from experiencing the fullness of God's joy and from growing intimately with Jesus. In common with anger and worry, impatience grabs control over us when we lose our focus on Christ and look only to ourselves, someone else, and circumstances. Joy is stolen from our hearts from our hearts when it prevents us and others from exercising compassion and deeper care for one another. Productivity and fulfillment disappear from any group, team, or enterprise if employees or team members are frequently expressing impatience with one another.

Impatience is usually the child of a selfish heart. If I am impatient with you, it is most likely that I am feeling thwarted in accomplishing my agenda or in getting my way. Impatience can suddenly break out at a person through my heart—sometimes surprising me as I think, *Why did I say that or act like that? I didn't think I was feeling so frustrated today!* The country music group Alabama popularized a song that included these words:

> I'm always in a hurry to get things done
> I rush and rush until life's no fun
> All I really gotta do is live and die,
> But, I'm in a hurry and I don't know why.[xi]

The words from this song capture the essence of life for many of us. We allow most things to clutter our lives and then we frantically attempt to juggle too many things in one 24-hour day.

DISCOVERING YOUR WEAPON FOR WINNING OVER IMPATIENCE—A DOUBLE-EDGED SWORD

The great news is this: there is a great weapon that can give you the upper hand in the battle against impatience. Of course, it is patience. The Bible reveals patience as a *"fruit of the Spirit"*—a characteristic of the Lord Jesus Christ Himself (Galatians 5:22). To develop patience is to develop a quality of Christ in your life. A patient Christian will reveal much more of the beauty and grace of Christ to those with whom he or she works. Patience has two sides—it is a double-edged weapon.

1. **Active side of patience**—The Greek word *makrathumia* means to be 'large' in self-restraint or self-control. It refers to your ability to restrain yourself in specific situations or relationships. With God's help, you can choose to restrain yourself in acting gracefully toward someone who has wronged you. It is an active response.

In the early days of my work as a church pastor, I spent so much time working with other people and their families that I often neglected my own. So many wives might have left their husbands and asked for a divorce. But I had two things in my favor: our initial commitment to a lifelong marriage and the amazing patience of my wife Sandra. With three young children who were very close in age, Sandra displayed great self-restraint and chose to express her love when what I really deserved was justified anger. After many years of marriage, I have learned valuable lessons because of Sandra's use of the active side of patience.

During the early hours of one day, two young men were hurrying to reach Vancouver's airport for an international flight. They apparently passed a man in a pickup truck and kept moving ahead. With a total lack of restraint, the truck driver became furious, increased his speed, and ran the vehicle of the two younger guys off the road. Not satisfied with this result, the infuriated driver decided to return to the two young men, who were now standing by the side of the road. One of the young men escaped, but the other was instantly killed by a man who demonstrated a lethal result of extreme impatience. This action destroyed one life and cancelled any joy or fulfillment in the person who survived the ordeal. They were traveling to see family members. Instead, the surviving man will probably suffer nightmares of this experience for years to come.

This word for active patience is used in the Bible for God. *"[The Lord] is patient with you, not wanting anyone to perish"* (2 Peter 3:9). Think about patience from God's point of view. God did not make us as robotic creatures who automatically do everything exactly as He desires. He made us as human beings who have the capacity to think, reason, feel, and choose what to say or do or where to go. In this capacity, each of us is created in the image of God (Genesis 1:27). God wants us to love Him deeply, but He also wants us to make our own decision about loving and serving Him. Having creatures with a will of their own—now with a selfish tendency due to the entrance of sin into humankind—makes it all the more amazing that God would be so patient with our rebellion and wayward living.

It is also used for people. *"Be patient, then, brothers, until the Lord's coming"* (James 5:7). You might say, "It's easier for God to be patient in an active sense—to restrain Himself in His response toward me. But how can I be patient until Jesus returns? That might mean that I have to restrain and control myself in a wide variety of situations throughout my life." Exactly! The great news is—you don't have to develop and express this kind of patience all on your own. As the Apostle Paul declared to followers of Jesus in the old Greek city of Philippi, *"It is God who works in you to will and to act for his good purpose!"* (Philippians 2:13). Isn't this incredible? You can have all the patience you need as you put your complete dependence and trust in the God who is patience personified.

Imagine how the application of this truth empowers you to be a more understanding and encouraging spouse, parent, or friend. Think of greater safety on the highways and streets of our neighborhoods. During the darkest winter night, I stopped on a snow-covered city street for a red light. Amazingly, several cars made left turns in front of me on an amber, and then a red light. With a green light, I proceeded forward, not expecting any vehicle to cross in front of me. Suddenly, a pickup driver was so impatient that he tried to make the left turn—perhaps the fourth vehicle on a red light! I tried to break on the slippery street. The other driver stopped and reversed to the wait line. I missed hitting him by two inches! I prayed a prayer of thanks to God.

2. **Passive side of patience**—The Greek word *hupomeno* means to 'abide under' or a willingness to bear hardship or criticism—in a biblical sense, to bear hardship for Christ. To bear up under such pressure is more than possible if you are willing to give your whole life over to God on a daily basis. It means that you are truly at peace with God in your heart and that you are ready to approach everything in life through the 'lens' of God. Seeing people and situations through the eyes of God will give you much greater patience in dealing with someone who really needs your help at a given moment. Personal acceptance that God really is all-powerful, all-knowing, and compassionate can then empower you to treat even your worst critic with patience, love,

70

and discernment! How? By allowing this awesome God to work freely through you for His glory and your good.

If you dare to follow Jesus with all your heart, you can expect that others will 'hate you.' But stand firm and patiently endure for Jesus (John 15:18-20). Jesus told us to expect hardship when we follow Him. As a disciple of Jesus, Peter warned us to expect Satan's attacks. *"He prowls around like a roaring lion, looking for some victim to devour. Take a firm stand against him, and be strong in your faith"* (1 Peter 5:8-9, NLT). God allows you to endure such pressure because it will strengthen you to become even more effective in encouraging others and influencing them to embrace God and His gift of life. Keep God's long-term plan in mind—that He is building a family of Christ-followers to enjoy Him, live with Him, and display His incredible glory forever!

> Be glad for all God is planning for you. Be patient in trouble, and always be prayerful. When God's children are in need, be the one to help them out. And get into the habit of inviting guests home for dinner or, if they need lodging, for the night. (Romans 12:12-13, NLT)

But you may protest, "I can't invite just anybody into my house—can I? How can I know whom God wants me to influence, inspire, and encourage" The book of Proverbs provides an answer: *"A patient man has great understanding"* (Proverbs 14:29). It is easy to get defensive when someone criticizes you. But as I have learned over a long period of time, if I listen to my critics, I can develop a deeper understanding of myself and others. *"If you reject criticism, you only harm your-*

self; but if you listen to correction, you grow in understanding" (Proverbs 15:32, NLT).

Dan (not his real name) regularly attended the gym where I also worked out. I would observe him working on his exercise routines—usually alone. He rarely talked to anyone and very few ever talked to him—except when absolutely necessary. I intentionally took time to greet him and have brief chats. Before this happened, I would pray for Dan, asking God for wisdom and understanding to help me make a difference in his life.

One day, Dan noticed me in the gym and approached me with these exact words:

> "Stewart, I'm living in darkness. Can you
> help me?"

What followed was a process in exercising great patience to understand a young man whose life was incredibly crippled and damaged by layers of accumulated negative experiences. As I asked Dan about his life, he unfolded a story of abuse, betrayal, and abandonment. His closest family members were now in jail, he said. He had been adopted by another family. One day, I went to his apartment to meet with him. On my way, I felt a heavy oppression come over me. It occurred to me that I had not asked some of my team leaders to pray for me as I traveled to his residence. On entering his apartment, I saw a weird, dark object decorating the walls. The opposition of Satan was very apparent. I gave him a New Testament and challenged him to rid himself of all things that conveyed spiritual darkness and evil. Before he could follow Jesus, he had to get rid of evil, and emblems of evil, as well as anything that could prevent him from 'seeing' and completely trusting in Jesus as His Savior and director of his life.

Dan's dramatic story continues. I would never have been a part of his story without growing in the patience and inner personal security that God provides. From a growing sense of security in my own life, I was more motivated to connect with, understand, and walk beside Dan so that he could finally see more clearly the choices before him.

But what steps can we take to actually experience more of a patient mindset in our lives? Let's look at several steps that are both essential and achievable in our lives as we work with others.

Practical Steps for Individuals and Small Groups

1. Take the patience test at the beginning of this chapter. How patient are you? Discuss with your P.I.E. or small group.

2. What is the intended warning in the quotation from 1 Timothy 4:16: "Watch yourself and your teaching"? What are the consequences of focusing on **doing** while neglecting who you are **becoming**?

3. Increasing patience is a logical fruit which emerges out of a clean (Christ-like) heart and growing spiritual maturity. Describe the scenario in a normal day in your life if you discipline yourself to **guard your heart**. Read Proverbs 4:20-27.

4. Who you are becoming fully influences and informs your responses to others around you in any situation. If this is true, how are you responding to the demanding or difficult persons in your life? What does your response say about the progress of (or lack of) patient character in you?

5. Are you a hurried person? What are some of the indicators informing you of this fact?

6. The word 'patience' has both and **active** and **passive** components. Define these terms. How can you develop these in your own life so that you can truly encourage others?

7. There is a quotation from Proverbs 14:29: *"A patient man has great understanding."* What benefits can someone receive if you have a great understanding of him or her?

CHAPTER NINE
Imitation: Experience Patience Through a Transformed Life

I t is said that imitation is the sincerest form of flattery. But imitation of Jesus is the sincerest form of praise to God. To make *intentional encouragement* a way of life, rather than a series of random actions, you need to make patience a lasting quality of your character. Patience is a central quality of Jesus. To instill His patience in your mind, heart, and whole life requires that you intentionally plan time to be *with* Jesus every day. The more you allow Jesus to express His patient heart through you, the more you will think like Him and reflect Him in the way you live life. How can you do this? Here are seven ways to make patience a more lasting quality in your life:

1. IMITATE JESUS BY YIELDING YOURSELF TO GOD AND THE HOLY SPIRIT

Real followers of Jesus need to be filled with the Holy Spirit (Ephesians 5:18). When the Holy Spirit fills you, He is in charge of your life. He directs your life, guiding you in all your decisions, empowering you in all your responses to life issues, and in the process making you like Jesus. It is the work of the Holy Spirit to exalt Jesus and to form the character of Christ in you as you obey Him by faith.

When Jesus came to earth the first time, He intentionally lived within the limits of human flesh. Because He became an authentic human being, Jesus lived and ministered to people's needs and served God the Father by the power of the Holy Spirit (Matthew 3:16, 4:1). It is this same Holy Spirit whom He sends to live within every person who receives Jesus into their hearts by faith (John 14:16-17). That is why we are told that we must allow the Holy Spirit of God to develop in us the fruit of the Spirit, which are the character qualities of Jesus:

> But the fruit of the Spirit is love, joy, peace, patience, kindness, goodness, faithfulness, gentleness and self-control. (Galatians 5:22-23)

It is obvious that patience has many 'family members' that compose a Christ-like character. Yes, this is the very character of Jesus that enabled Him to take the time, whatever the circumstance, to notice a person in need, and to come alongside such a person, connecting, empowering, and transforming him or her for the glory of God. Make the practice of patience the core of your prayer as you seek to grow in all nine qualities. Imitate Jesus by:

- Keeping your eyes on God's ultimate goal for you.
- Determining to love and please God in all you do.

- Living in sync with God's word through
  your thoughts, words, and actions.

Beware of the game so many adults play—a game reflected in the following story. A young boy was riding in the car with his parents. After getting him to sit down and fasten his seatbelt, the parents assumed all was well. Suddenly, the boy removed his seatbelt and stood up in the moving car. The boy was commanded to sit down and fasten his seatbelt. He obeyed—in part. He responded, "I am sitting down, but in my heart I am standing up!"

Start practicing the patience of Jesus towards your spouse, your parent, or your child! Begin where you are.

2. WAIT FOR GOD'S TIMING

Impatience and acting too quickly on a matter is a sure sign that you are focused on yourself and not on God. You are looking at your limitations rather than God in His awesome power. Timing is crucial to all key life situations. One of those situations involve you driving along the road. Timing ensures relatively smooth driving. But wrong timing may mean collision with another vehicle. What is needed? **Patience!** Patience to slow down for an amber light at the intersection. Patience to slow down to a stop for the red light. Patience to allow for reckless behavior from other drivers or for slippery road surfaces. In my city, too many drivers have the awful and dangerous habit of racing up to a light in the city and then slamming hard on the brakes because they have to stop for the stop sign or the traffic light. Many accidents occur because drivers cannot or will not stop in time.

A **powerful lesson on timing** is provided by Saul, the first king of ancient Israel (1 Samuel 13). Saul was asked to wait for God's prophet Samuel before providing an offering on an altar and seeking God's counsel through worship. Meanwhile, enemies of Israel, the Philistines, were marshalling their military forces for an invasion of Israel. Pressure and tension mounted, exacerbated by increasing numbers of Saul's troops deserting him at a critical time. If you forget about God's power and focus only on the power of your human enemy, as King Saul did, you can identify with Saul's fear and desire to take matters into his own hands.

Saul was told to wait one week until Samuel returned. Saul waited six days and most of the seventh day. He was obedient to God most of the time—but he did not wait for the complete seven days. Should Saul be congratulated for almost total obedience? Obviously God said, No! *"'You acted foolishly', Samuel said"* (1 Samuel 13:13). The word 'foolish' translates as to lack moral and spiritual understanding. Here is a crucial step for developing real patience in your life:

> Understand that wise discernment and understanding arises out of 100% obedience to the word of God!

If Saul had waited just a few more minutes, as God's word required of him, he would have received the full blessing of God and an extended successful rule over the nation. Like Saul, we are called to actively wait on God and act promptly with faith on His directions!

If you trust God for discernment and understanding of all situations, trials, and challenges that you face, you will be more patient both with yourself and with the person near you who needs your help. There is good reason for the familiarity of the phrase "the wisdom of Solomon." Faced with the enormous task of leading a whole nation, the new king,

Solomon, prayed and asked God for wisdom to govern. In response, God gave him wisdom and understanding so that, in his early years, Solomon displayed the wisdom of God, expressed with amazing patience. All Israel responded with awe when King Solomon made a judgment in the case of the two prostitutes (1 Kings 3:16-28). It was more than a display of wisdom and patience—it was God's **majesty in motion** through Solomon!

3. MEDITATE ON GOD'S NATURE

Take time to read Biblical truth about the person of God and stop to reflect on the awesome qualities of God's character—especially the qualities of grace and patience. Psalm 103:8-13 is a reminder of the amazing patience of God with you. Focusing on this can greatly expand your patience for others in your family and in your community. Notice the majesty of God as He seeks to work in your heart, drawing you ever closer in His loving embrace, if you will allow Him to do so.

> The Lord is merciful and gracious; he is **slow to get angry** and full of unfailing love. He will not constantly accuse us, nor remain angry forever. He has not punished us for all our sins, nor does be deal with us as we deserve. For his **unfailing love** toward those who fear him is as great as the height of the heavens above the earth. He has removed our rebellious acts as far away from us as the east is from the west. The Lord is like a father to his children, **tender and compassionate** to those who fear Him. (Psalm 103:8-13, emphasis mine).

The highlighted words above are all qualities necessary for patience in our lives. Although they are descriptive of God, they also describe those in whom God lives by His Holy Spirit. They are not instant qualities, but qualities that Jesus will develop in you as you spiritually grow and allow Him to become more and more of what Rick Warren calls "the resident and the president" of your heart.

How can you avoid getting angry about something or with someone? How can you love without failing? How can a friend or a stranger count on tenderness and compassion from you? It is possible only by seeing that person through the eyes of God and trusting God to soften and tenderize your heart toward that person in need of encouragement. After all, the Lord is *"full of tenderness and mercy"* (James 5:11, NLT).

4. THINK OF THE RESULTS OF PATIENCE APPLIED

A farmer knows that he or she could not survive, let alone thrive, in growing grain or raising livestock without lots of patience. The challenges of weather, pests, or disease can so easily and quickly test one's patience. Yet the rewards of patience can yield bumper crops, products to sell, and a good income. If you plant a garden of flowers or vegetables at your residence, you know that patience is essential for achieving good results.

The Bible also reminds us of Job. "The patience of Job" has become a famous phrase for good reason. Job was an authentic man in history who stayed the course and hung onto God even when he lost his children, his health, and his wealth. Faced with the urging of his wife to "curse God and die," Job was patient with God even though he neither understood what God was doing nor the full reality of spiritual warfare. The result was that God blessed Job much more than ever—with family, health, and economic blessings! (Job 42:12, James 5:11)

In the same way, think of what patience can do in the way you treat your spouse or children. Instead of getting into a rage over being cut off on the road, or of being deceived or mistreated by a neighbor of friend, think of what patience can do both in you and in the heart of the other person if patience with grace is allowed to work!

5. CULTIVATE HOPE IN YOUR LIFE

In any circumstance, you need hope. Hope is **confident expectation** for your future. Since God is the only one who can guarantee your future, keep seeking Him and growing closer to Him so that you'll see life through the eyes of God.

> I pray that God, who gives you hope, will keep you happy and full of peace as you believe in him. (Romans 15:13, NLT)

6. PRACTICE THE DISCIPLINE OF STILLNESS IN YOUR LIFE

Learn from someone who spent years enduring hatred, accusations, and threats. King David would have lost his sanity in those earlier years if he had not taken time to be still before the Lord. Stillness quiets and stabilizes an anxious, fretful mind, especially when it is focused on God.

> Be still before the Lord and wait patiently for him. (Psalm 37:7)

The word 'still' refers here to silence. Stop talking and thinking about yourself so that you can focus on God and hear Him clearly when he communicates to you. Peter had to learn this lesson as a disciple of Jesus when he experienced the blazing glory of Jesus on what is called the Mount of Transfiguration. Peter was reminded by God to focus only on Jesus and listen to Him alone. In our rapidly changing world of communication devices, it takes great effort and discipline to remove ourselves from the cell phone and the iPod for just a few minutes to be still before God.

The result of stillness is mentioned by the prophet Isaiah:

> [The Lord] will keep in perfect peace him whose mind is steadfast, because he trusts in you. (Isaiah 26:3)

The practice of such stillness before God leads to inner peace, stability, and strength. Many of us spend too much time rushing about and engaging in activity without really accomplishing anything of lasting value. Take ten minutes for seven consecutive days to concentrate your mind first on the verse above, and then on the person of God Himself. Reflect on the arms of God surrounding you and lifting you up. In doing so, you will discover that God is equipping you to refresh and strengthen others during the course of the day ahead of you.

At one time, the Discovery Channel had a report about the dangers of rip currents for swimmers. They specifically reported on the challenges faced by swimmers at famous Bondi Beach in Sydney, Australia. Rip currents are powerful currents of water that can suddenly pull a swimmer out to sea without warning. Some beaches have a bowl-like configuration in which waves crash onto the beach only to be funneled into a narrow, concentrated current that rushes out to sea, sucking all in its path out with it. How do you survive such a danger? Rip current expert Dr. Rob Brander recommends that swimmers literally go with the flow. Above all, relax before calling for help from beach guards. It seems that most swimmers who drown do so in a rip current panic. The same dynamic is at work in your daily life. There are rip currents of temptations, problems, conflicts, or addictions that threaten to suck you away from the safe haven of the shore. But relax and rest in Jesus the Son of God, and call on Him who is able to not only save you spiritually, but empower you daily!

> Be still before the Lord and wait patiently for him; do not fret when men succeed in their ways, when they carry out their wicked schemes. Refrain from anger and turn from wrath; do not fret—it leads only to evil. (Psalm 37:7-8)

The discipline of stillness anchors your mind and emotions in God. It sharpens your hearing and sensitivity to the Holy Spirit of God.

In early Israel, a young boy named Samuel was dedicated to the service of God by his mother Hannah. So Samuel grew up within the context of serving the Lord in His temple. One night, Samuel heard a voice calling his name. Samuel went to ask the temple priest Eli whether he had called him. By the fourth call, Samuel realized, with Eli's help, that this was the voice of the Lord. God waits until He has your full attention. This is how God responded to Samuel and Moses (1 Samuel 3:10-11, Exodus 3:4). Stillness and cultivating the skill of real listening builds your patience so that you can manage yourself and meet the needs of others, even in trying circumstances.

7. BUILD STRUCTURAL FORMS FOR PATIENCE AND ALLOW GOD TO FILL THEM[xii]

Before pouring concrete, workers would prepare the ground and build wooden forms in which to pour the concrete. The wooden structural forms would hold the concrete mix in place until it hardened, producing the desired result of a new sidewalk. The form enabled the workers to achieve the final result.

In the same way, you need certain disciplines to act as structural forms in your life so that you can achieve your desired final result—Christ-like patience toward God, with yourself, and with others. What kinds of forms are needed? One is a set time each day for slow deliberate reading of the Bible, God's holy inspired word. Don't rush through it. Make time in your daily schedule so that you can personally worship God through focusing your thoughts on Him. Even if you are not a good singer, sing through some songs of praise to God. Include some of the psalms—putting your own tune into it if you are not aware of an existing one. Sing out loud in a quiet place. Prepare your own heart and mind to receive a truth or truths from your designated reading for that day.

Before you read, ask the Lord to guide you by His Holy Spirit and reveal to you a sin in your life, an action you need to take, someone you need to encourage, or a principle you need to apply in your life. Then start reading by faith that God will speak to you through one or more verses of text. When you are challenged, inspired, or convicted by a verse or two, use this time to memorize it. Write them on a small card that can fit into your purse or pocket. Look at it and review it when you get a spare moment at home, workplace, or even when working out at the gym. This will not only help develop patience in you, but spiritual sensitivity to others and a strengthening of Christ-awareness in your life.

One day, I took a 3x5 card with the following words into the gym.

> Yet I am always with you;
> you hold me by my right hand.
> You guide me with your counsel,
> and afterward you will take me into glory.
> Whom have I in heaven but you?
> And earth has nothing I desire besides you.
> My flesh and my heart may fail,
> but God is the strength of my heart
> and my portion forever.
> (Psalm 73:23-26)

When I began to work through the cardio part of my exercise routine, my card was placed in front of me. One of my gym friends, who is not a follower of Jesus, noticed the card and asked, "What do you have there, Stewart?"

*I told him that the words were verses from the Bible that I had chosen from my quiet time with God that morning, and I explained that I was memorizing them. Then, he asked, "What does it say?" In response, I read the above verses. In reading this, I silently prayed that God would use His powerful word to communicate Jesus to my friend's heart. We then had a great conversation about what it means to become a Christian. I wanted him to experience lasting encouragement through a faith relationship with Jesus Christ! It is tremendously helpful and empowering to know that the words "God is the strength of my heart" can also read, "God is the **encouragement** of my heart"!*

86

Practical Steps for Individuals and Small Groups

1. It is said that we need the patience of Job. To be more accurate, we need the patience of Jesus. Review the seven steps to developing patience in your life. What steps are necessary as priorities in your life at this moment?

2. Grace is often defined as the favor of God toward us even though we don't deserve it as sinners. Yet we desperately need it. Identify one or two persons in your sphere of influence who need the touch of God's grace through you.

3. It is an awesome experience to know the timing of God in any given situation. Read 1 Samuel 13. What can you learn about patience and trust through this true story? Notice that God called Saul to be completely (not almost completely) obedient.

4. How does meditation on the nature of God help you to develop a patient character?

5. What structural forms can you implement in your life as fertile ground for growing in Christ-like patience?

CHAPTER TEN
Dry Dock Repairs
for Lasting Performance

Attempting to make progress on a leaky ship is sure to give you a sinking feeling! To be an encourager and to intentionally encourage the heart of a person, you need to cultivate not only real joy and patience in your life, but also peace. Many people are worriers. Are you a worrier? Until you begin to make progress over a worried mindset, you will not be secure and internally stable enough to encourage someone else over an extended period of time.

It is not enough to plug small leaks in your life. That is like trying to repair a tiny hole in a ship instead of putting it into dry dock for a complete overhaul and restoration—from the inside-out.

Others have noted that the *Titanic* was never in danger of sinking while it rode on the surface of the ocean. The danger emerged only when water began to pour into the ship through the hole punctured by an iceberg. Like the ship taking on water, once you allow worry to take up residence in your heart, you begin to feel weighed down and depleted of energy and strength needed to overcome even the smallest of life's challenges.

An unknown poet wrote:

> All the water in the world
> However hard it tried,
> Could never sink a ship
> Unless it got inside
> All the hardships of this world
> Might wear you pretty thin,
> But they won't hurt you one least bit
> Unless you let them in.

It is obvious that you cannot take someone else to a level or destination that you have never achieved. In the same way, one who worries cannot lift and inspire another person to an experience of peace and healthy confidence. Worry is an enemy of personal peace and it easily spreads in your family or group like a tiny spark setting a forest on fire. Once you make it an ingrained habit practiced over years of your life, it is difficult to live as an encouraged person because your worry prevents the growth of true inner peace. To deal with worry and restore real Christ-like peace in your heart, you need to first understand what worry is all about. Most of us worry over situations or persons at various times. However, worry that becomes deeply rooted as a chronic condition in us needs to be eliminated before it produces irreversible damage.

IDENTIFYING WORRY AND HOW IT HURTS ME

Jesus warns about worry and its effect on our lives. He identifies three aspects of worry in the context of teaching His disciples how to live.

Worry is Distracting. Jesus said, *"Do not worry about your life, what you will eat or drink"* (Matthew 6:25). The Greek word for worry here is *merimnao* and it has the meaning of 'distracting attention,' of 'becoming overextended in different directions at once.' It is like having your hair being pulled in different directions at the same time—it is painful. Your mind is in overload as you think about this problem and that problem. You feel as if you are coming apart. It is the state of your mind when you are unable to settle down and focus on the main thing in front of you. Have you ever lost sleep at night because your mind was in turmoil as you tensed up, thinking about one issue after another? When that happens, you know that your mind is not focused on God, but on your own limitations and inabilities.

That is why Jesus commands those who follow Him to **stop worrying and focus instead on God, who provides all that you need!**

Worry is Devouring. Jesus reminds us that we cannot add any extra time to our lives or enrich ourselves in any way by worrying. It seems that the word 'worry' comes from an old Anglo-Saxon word, 'wolf.' The meaning is clear. Worry acts like a wolf when you allow it to take up permanent residence in your heart and mind. Like a ravenous wolf, worry will devour you from within. You begin to weaken from within. Your stomach churns, your mind feels numb, and it feels harder to mentally process information, conversations, and decisions. Eventually, ulcers may appear in your stomach and your basic health begins to suffer. Worrying is telling you that you are not in the right relationship with God at that moment. You are relying on yourself instead of trusting God by faith. Worry says, "I cannot do this" or "I cannot deal with an offended spouse, friend, or neighbor." The fact is that God always gives you a task, mission, or vision that you cannot do on your own. You need His power by His Spirit, *always!*

Worry is Doubting. When you worry, you are doubting God. Now, many of us doubt at times. To doubt is to express our humanity—that is, our human nature distorted by sin. But God views our doubting, with respect to His word and promises, as sin. For example, when Zechariah received word from God that he and his wife would become parents in their old age, he doubted. In response, God did not allow him to speak until after the baby's birth, when Zechariah gave the baby the name God had told him. God will not strike all doubters so that they cannot speak, but God was making the point that His word was true.

Many of the original disciples and past followers of Jesus experienced doubt. Nevertheless, God wants to help you diminish your doubt and increase your faith. God wants you to live in confidence that He can supply every genuine need that you have. In a world that is increasingly connected, and also unstable in its economic, financial, and moral foundations, it is crucial to be sure about your relationship with God. Jesus refers to those who, while claiming to follow Jesus, act like those who did not believe in God (Matthew 6:31-32). They panic and act rashly because they do not know how they will pay the mortgage, pay their basic bills, and live from day to day. They go beyond that to worry about next month or next year. Jesus encourages those who trust in him as their Savior, "Don't act like unbelievers or pagans. Believe that God really cares for you and will supply your need." Doubting also discourages others around you and weakens their ability and yours to make wise decisions and appropriate actions. What is the solution? How can you deal with the distracting, devouring, doubting characteristics of worry?

HOW CAN I DEFEAT THIS ENEMY OF WORRY?

The solution is to allow God to fully direct your life and allow His peace to fill your mind each day. The Bible is clear about the source of real lasting peace that is essential for you to experience encouragement and to encourage others. Speaking to those who had turned from sinful, selfish living and who , trusted in Jesus for salvation, the Apostle Paul said:

> Since we have been justified through faith, we have peace with God through our Lord Jesus Christ. (Romans 5:1)

To experience peace requires **peace with God**—that is, the decision to invite Jesus into my life as my personal Savior to deal with my past sins, present living, and future hope. It also means that I choose to invite Jesus to be the director of my life. The Bible says that until I receive Jesus as my Savior, I live as an "enemy" of God (Romans 5:10). When I confess my sin and invite Jesus to take over my heart, I am reconciled to God and His peace begins to change my heart and mind. The Bible says that Jesus Himself is our peace (Ephesians 2:14). Now the life of God can flow though me to you—it is the majesty of God's goodness being expressed through my humanity to you!

Once you experience **peace with God,** you can then know the **peace of God.** To have peace with God is to be in right relationship with Him, to be in sync or in step with God. This enables Jesus, the Savior, to become the full director of your life and to live out His divine life through your unique personality. As you allow God to direct your life, He begins to fill your life—your heart, mind, and emotions—with His peace. In the New Testament, the word 'peace' is defined as **harmony in relationship.** It means that out of your harmonious relationship with the Lord, you then have the ability to relate in harmony with others around you. In the Old Testament, the Hebrew word for peace, *Shalom*, means **wholeness.** Instead of inner turmoil, you experience a sense of wholeness, stability, and genuine confidence of being in Christ and Christ being in you.

Living in close proximity to someone else confirms the presence or absence of genuine inner peace—a sign that God is at work within you. As you learn to rest in God, your capacity to grow as an intentional encourager to your spouse, family, and neighbor increases dramatically. Inner peace through faith in Jesus is so crucial to a healthy and fruitful life that we are commanded not to worry. Therefore we need to pay careful attention to words of the Apostle Paul to Christians at the Greek city of Philippi—words also given to us by God:

> Do not be anxious about anything, but in everything, by prayer and petition, with thanksgiving, present your requests to God. And the peace of God, which transcends all understanding, will guard your hearts and your minds in Christ Jesus. (Philippians 4:6-7)

The word for 'guard' has a military background, indicating God's power to protect you with a deep abiding peace in the midst of the instabilities of life in our world. This inner peace through Jesus empowers you to encourage others deeply.

HOW CAN YOU USE GOD'S PEACE TO OVERCOME WORRY?

1. Choose not to worry. God commands you to reject worry. *"Do not be anxious about anything..."* God has given you the ability to think and to choose. The word translated as 'anxiety' in this verse has the sense of accumulating a series of anxious thoughts over a period of time until it becomes an ingrained habit—worry!

2. Begin to list the specific things that make you worried or anxious. The only way to untangle the messy web of anxious thoughts is to take an in-depth look at the past trains of thought in your mind. As you list them, prayerfully give them over to God. God will take away these destructive mental burdens as you focus on Him and meditate on the truth of the Bible, His holy word (1 Peter 5:7). It took much time to build up your mountain of worry. It will take more time to dismantle it. When I feel anxious, I seek to mentally review awesome truth (like the following):

> You will keep in perfect peace him whose
> mind is steadfast because he trusts in You.
> (Isaiah 26:3)

3. Make God the **priority of your life!** Jesus taught that to be His disciple, you need to "… *seek first [God's] kingdom*" (Matthew 6:33). The kingdom of God is the area or realm of God's rule. The word 'first' has the sense of first in order or rank. In essence, it implies that God is my number one priority, which influences and shapes every other lesser priority in my life.

For example, you may say, "My spouse or my family is most important in my life." However, if you want your family, spouse, or friend to really have God's very best for their lives, you must put God first in your mind, heart, and life. Long ago, it was King David who said, *"I have set the Lord always before me"* (Psalm 16:8). If you seek always to honor God, He will honor you (1 Samuel 2:30). When God is at home and directing in your heart, He will reveal and shower His unfailing love through you to your wife, husband, or friend! It never fails! When Jesus Christ is first in your life, those closest to you will benefit enormously as He works His nurturing grace through your unique personality. Married couples who put God as *the* priority in their lives will increasingly treat each other as the most important person of all. It is as if the other person were more important than you. When you have the mind of Jesus, that is how you will see and treat your spouse or friend! (Philippians 2:3,5)

Pray about Everything!

> Don't worry about anything: instead, pray
> about everything. (Philippians 4:6, NLT)

This is a word for comprehensive prayer. This requires an attitude of continuous prayer. Talk to God. Think about pleasing Him. Thank Him for every breath that you breathe. Walk and pray. Think and pray. Sing and pray God's written word back to him. Take words such as Psalm 23. If you have already given your heart and life in faith to Christ as your Savior, pray like this:

Lord, you are my shepherd. As one of your sheep, one of your adopted children, I will not lack any necessary thing to accomplish your will here on earth. You have promised that you will supply my every need including rest and renewed strength (in "green pastures") as I wait on you in faith, you promise to restore my soul, spirit, emotions, and my whole being. If I am willing to obey you, you promise to guide me to make right decisions and take appropriate actions. In this way, I can live righteously and in honor before everyone I meet. Even when I face the darkest valleys and most difficult situations in life, you will be there for me! I can trust you to rescue me and protect me from all evil and destructive influences until I have accomplished your purposes for me. I feel saturated with your presence[xiii] *and I am overflowing with joy! Even those who oppose me will see your blessings on me. Lord, I now know beyond any doubt that you will pursue me with your goodness and unfailing love every day of my life. I now know that I can live daily in a spirit of continuing hope and anticipation of life eternal with you when all sin and death will be wiped away!*

Imagine how much joy will fill your life when you pray like this to God. Think of how much the written word of God will equip you to face the difficult times and the good times. The attitude of prayer is followed by a more specific word for prayer: petition (Philippians 4:6). This is the word for 'bringing to God your very specific needs.' You can be sure that God will hear and receive your very specific requests if you are constantly walking with Him in a more comprehensive spirit or attitude of prayer. None of us does this in a perfect way. But when you stray from God, act on your own, or fail to trust Him continuously, ask His forgiveness and go on walking in faith with Him.

Plan specific times and a place for prayer and seeking the Lord. You need to do this, or else you will allow the many distractions of life to crowd out your prayer life. Develop the attitude and mindset of praying and actively trusting God at any time and all times. Let a prayerful attitude energize your work and inspire your employer. Let it encourage your co-workers, lift your family, and affirm your spouse.

4. Practice a gratitude attitude. Realize that you need to be grateful for every breath that you breathe. All blessing come from God. There is nothing worse than being ungrateful. If you complain and worry, your strength decreases and others are discouraged by your very presence. It is amazing how an attitude of thanksgiving can lift someone without even saying a word. Such a spirit energizes your body and conveys to others that you truly care.

> In everything, by prayer and petition, with thanksgiving, present your requests to God. (Philippians 4:6)

I understand that the word 'thank' comes from an old Anglo-Saxon word meaning 'think'—to **thank is to think.** Never take the gifts of God for granted.[xiv] Understand that you do not have the right to all that God has given you. It is an immense privilege to have the gifts of physical and spiritual life. Live life with an attitude of amazement for the gracious redemptive way that the Lord treats you. As you take time to think about all of God's **blessings**, let your thinking lead to thanking Him.

Make every effort to keep a supply of thank you cards to share with those who have touched and encouraged you in some way. E-mails, phone calls, visits, and cards are all ways that should be used at various times to intentionally encourage others and honor God at the same time. When you serve others in this way, you are demonstrating the biblical meaning of majesty—the greatness of God. You are then able to represent Him to others—this is **majesty in motion!**

The result of gratitude will be an overflowing heart, an energized body, and a peaceful mind.

> The peace of God, which transcends all understanding, will guard your hearts and your minds in Christ Jesus. (Philippians 4:7)

If you are becoming more deeply motivated by joy, directed by Christ-like patience, and persevering in the long run by the indwelling peace of God, then you possess a solid foundation for living a life of encouragement. Out of this encouraging life, you will be empowered to more deeply encourage others around you.

Practical Steps for Individuals and Small Groups

1. Repairs to broken and leaky ships are made in dry dock. Ships continually need repairs and rebuilding so that they can travel on the water instead of sinking. God is in the wonderful work of repairing leaky people. D.L. Moody once referred to Christians as leaky vessels who needed to stay continually under the fountain of the Holy Spirit.

    *   Worry can be defined as a leaking out of inner confidence from your heart. The result is that you quickly sink under your worry rather than living on top of it.

    *   Do you worry? Can you describe examples of how a specific worry robbed you of strength to resolve an issue and prevented you from really helping someone else in their need?

2. From this chapter, identify three ways in which worry can hurt you. How have these affected your role as a wife or husband, mom or dad, leader or neighbor?

3. Peace **with** God and the peace **of** God are keys to winning over worry. Identify specific actions that you can take (ways that you can obey God) to actually experience such peace in your heart and life. Then you can share this with another in need. How

can you establish a network of support so that a healthy growing relationship with God and with faithful friends can make the difference?

4. Review the five steps for using God's peace to winning over worry. Identify your progress on these. Note that you *cannot* separate steps one to three. Choosing not to worry *must* be followed by identifying the causes of your worry and then giving them over to God as the absolute director of your life. This third step gives meaning and success to the first two. Meet with your P.I.E. to identify the specific needs for each of you regarding this.

5. Take time to pray over each worry as you trust God to remove them from the core of your mind. As you *breathe out* (expel) each worry by faith, *breathe in* (receive) by faith the peace of God already offered to you through Christ" (Philippians 4:6-7).

6. In addition to Philippians 4:6-7 and 1 Thessalonians 5:18, read Psalm 103 as a basis from which to develop a grateful or thankful attitude. List reasons for which you can thank God.

* You must be **grateful** and **joyful** before you can be truly **helpful** as an encourager in your circles of relationships.

PART THREE

THE INTENTIONALITY
OF ENCOURAGEMENT

CHAPTER ELEVEN
Developing Healthy Relationships

E ven if you are equipped to truly encourage others to spiritual maturity in Christ, it will not happen unless you make every effort to keep on growing and to reach out to others to help them to grow in Christ-likeness. As flawed and sinful human beings, we tend to stay in our comfort zones and focus on pleasing ourselves. Resist this urge and launch out! Someone noted that you need to keep moving forward and go out on a limb to reach the ripest fruit. About two thousand years ago, Paul, the brilliant Hebrew apostle of Christ, noted the spiritually riches of the church in Corinth, Greece. Yet he was alarmed by their selfishness, jealousy, and competitiveness. They, too, were following the path of least resistance and therefore neglected to encourage and inspire others to a passionate devotion to Jesus. That is why Paul urges them to make every effort to *intentionally* work together for the good of everyone. Speaking of the crucial importance of mutual encouragement and ministry in God's spiritual family, the church, Paul writes, "*Make every effort to keep the unity of the Spirit through the bond of peace*" (Ephesians 4:3)*.

You must **intend** to connect with and inspire others! It has been noted in the past that many men who are in prison have had very poor or non-existent relationships with their fathers. The role of a mother seems obviously important to most of us, but fathers have an equally vital role to play in the development of healthy sons and daughters.

Brandon was a fifteen-year-old teenager who ran away from home after arguing with his parents over a video game. Video games and a million other electronic distractions can so easily replace healthy interaction and relationships between children, teenagers, and their parents. Brandon's father admitted that he did not understand the world that his son and other kids lived in. After Brandon was found dead, his father said,

> As parents, we need to understand that world a bit more and maybe take more time and understand why our kids are involved in that world so much... and try to make them understand why, as parents, we find that hard to realize that they don't want to go outside and play sports and they'd rather be inside playing these games.[xv]

If you are a parent with children, take time to model God's love to them. Take time to love them by listening, supporting, and teaching them the importance of the long-term results over the shallow pleasures of the immediate. Jesus reminded many of those who followed him around that they were more interested in the physical food that he provided than in the deeper reality of eternal life (John 6:26-27). This same warning is found in Hebrews, when God reminds us of true heroes of the Christians faith who grew up to be champions with enormous impact on others because they refused to focus on questionable or fleeting pleasure. Instead, they opted for the rewards that can never fade away:

> Make sure that no one is immoral or godless like Esau. He traded his birthright as the oldest son for a single meal. (Hebrews 12:16, NLT)

Teach your children the importance of a healthy relationship with God. You're your reasonable expectations very clear to them. Help them to see the consequences of their actions as positive steps in growing solid Christ-like character—empowering, energizing, and protecting them in the long run.

Practical Steps for
Individuals and Small Groups

1. We all like to live in comfort zones. What personal disciplines can you practice daily so that your mind is more tuned to focus on the blessing and needs of others whom you will encounter?

2. Unless you are preparing yourself to understand and encourage others according to their needs, you will miss great opportunities God allows to cross your daily path. Recall Brandon in this chapter. Think of someone like Brandon who needs more of your quality encouragement and inspiration over a period of time. What can you do to encourage him or her today?

3. The role of fathers and mothers are truly necessary in the healthy development of a son or daughter's mental, social, sexual, emotional, and spiritual health. For those without one or both parents, mature Christian parents in Christ-centered churches have great opportunities to encourage and love them. Discuss with others the specific individuals who need your prayers, acts of kindness, and expressions of love. Cheer for them as if they were your own flesh and blood family.

4. Developing healthy relationships, both with God and with each other, is essential if a family is to reveal

God's love and grace to needy guests. What would a visitor see if they were visiting you and your family today?

CHAPTER TWELVE
Removing the Mask

BUILDING SOLID FOUNDATIONS FOR HEALTHY RELATIONSHIPS

Alife of *intentional encouragement* depends on your willingness to be totally honest with God, with yourself, and with others. Our larger culture in the western world allows and even encourages in some way the idea of glamour, outward appearance, and first impressions. Even in churches, especially in larger evangelical churches, the focus is on first impressions for the visitor or "seeker." Entertainers command big bucks and fans hang on every word they say while excitedly watching the latest moves, cosmetic changes, and lifestyles of their favorite stars. While working out in my favorite gym, I notice that males and females of all shapes and sizes fix their gaze on the ideal body shapes and fashion wear of the champions in glossy magazines! They are so concerned about how they look that they seem to neglect who they are and who they are becoming inside. It leads to a life that covers or masks reality. This is living without integrity—leading to unnecessary stress and decreasing your ability to lift one another up.

My early years were lived in a region where the tradition of "mummering" was practiced. Each year between Christmas and New Year, citizens of many towns and villages would dress in weird and often over-sized clothes and masks of different kinds. They would then walk from house to house as "mummers"—disguising themselves in masks and other voices and movements. The object was to keep the hosts guessing as to the identity of the visitors. There was storytelling and laughter, ending usually with tea and snacks at the end regardless as to who "won"—the hosts or the visitors! Great fun! But the idea was to wear a mask. That can be funny as a contrived act, but not as day to day living. There are always persons around you who urgently and deeply need a genuine encouraging friend with the mask removed.

How would you describe yourself? Are you living with or without a mask? A recent incident reminded my wife Sandra and I of the ease by which any of us can be caught up in living life or parts of our lives 'undercover.'

We had just purchased a house in an established neighborhood of our city. But the house inspection revealed that we needed a new furnace sooner rather than later. The inspector who confirmed this fact offered to give us a great deal on a new furnace—minus the 7% federal tax! What would we do? It seemed like a great opportunity to save some money, because this would be a very expensive item for us. But for me this was a no-brainer. I told the inspector that, as a Christian, I could not agree to such a deal. Avoiding tax would be dishonest in the sight of God. It would also be breaking the laws of our nation. Even if I didn't like the government taking more tax money from me, I would still pay all that was required of me and honor God by doing it.

The furnace inspector was shocked by my response and blurted out the words, "Why are there so many religions?" I explained that religion is the attempt of people to earn God's grace and favor by their own efforts. That is very different from receiving God's free gift of eternal life through personal faith in Jesus Christ. Real Christianity is not just a religion, but a relationship with God. This relationship is continuous and allows God to progressively change my character and attitude from the inside-out. This results in me becoming a genuine representative of God in all my activities and relationships in this world. That furnace man began to understand that many people wear masks. They pretend to be persons who act nice and obey the law, but who may be sinning and committing acts of dishonesty, manipulation, or deceit.

Integrity must form the foundation for the follower of Jesus to live and act as an influential intentional encourager. The dictionary defines integrity as the state of being "honest... complete... undivided."[xvi] In the Bible, God reminds us of the great importance of being a man, woman, teenager, or student of integrity.

Two events in the Bible illustrate how vital integrity is to God. In ancient Israel, a man named Achan seized a beautiful robe, along with silver and gold pieces during the battle of Jericho, hiding the items in the ground beneath his tent. This act was in complete disobedience to God's command. The sin of one person can affect a whole family, group, organization, or church. Achan's sin prevented the Israelites from moving forward until the sin was confessed and judgment was given.

> But the Israelites acted unfaithfully in re-
> gard to the devoted things; Achan... took
> some of them. So the Lord's anger burned
> against Israel. (Joshua 7:1)

Notice how the sin of Achan had damaged the whole nation in God's sight? That is why you must not allow a sin to
stay unresolved in your life. As soon as you are aware of a
sin, confess it to the Lord and turn away from that sinful
thought and action. Otherwise, you will hurt the spirit and
heart of another person instead of truly helping in the long
run. Achan was pretending that all was okay when he was
actually covering a sin. He was wearing a mask and his whole
family tragically paid for his sin.

A second incident involved a couple named Ananias and
Saphira. They were members of the church of Christ in the
first century. They acted dishonestly by pretending to be
great sacrificial givers to the church, when that was not true.
They gave money for God's work for sharing with those in
need. That is good. But they pretended that they gave *all* the
money from a completed land sale. They chose to give only
some of the money, but they coveted a reputation as great
givers. In so doing, they were wearing the mask and trying to
disguise their real motives before all the church members.
That is the same as being dishonest with God Himself. Lying
and making false representation to God's people is the same
as lying to Almighty God. That is the reason the Apostle Peter
gives this verdict:

> What made you think of doing such a
> thing? You have not lied to men but to
> God. (Acts 5:4)

111

Nothing of permanence or lasting quality emerges out of superficial impressions or hypocritical behavior. The right behavior arises out of a right relationship with the Lord. Jesus said that God the Father is looking for worshippers who will worship Him in spirit and in truth (John 4:24). People around you won't know how much you care until they know that you are real and genuine—from the inside-out. This is *integrity*. Integrity in character gives birth to intentionality in action and sets the stage for real lasting encouragement from your heart to another!

Practical Steps for Individuals and Small Groups

1. Do you wear masks? If you are concerned more with pleasing people than you are with pleasing God, you will put on an appearance or mask to please them (see Matthew 6:1-18).

2. Identify specific masks in your life and confess these to God—trusting Him to help you live a life of humility and integrity. Do you cover up or act dishonestly in:

    - Your marriage?
    - Your family?
    - Your business dealings?
    - Relationship with your neighbors?
    - In sports?
    - With fellow workers?
    - Your church?

3. Review Joshua 7:1. What effect can the sin of one person have on a whole church or group? How should the lesson in Joshua 7 help you to become much more intentional in practicing a life of honesty, responsibility to others, and ultimately, to God?

4. Ananias and Sapphira are a classic case of people trying to wear a mask and keep up appearances before others. What was their specific sin? Have you

been guilty of this? How can you prevent this attitude from arising in your heart?

CHAPTER THIRTEEN
Freedom from Addiction

Addiction may be defined as the experience of being controlled and dominated by a substance, person or attitude. In this respect, deeply rooted attitudes or mindsets involving factors such as anger, bitterness, or jealousy can be addictive.

Once such attitudes take hold in a person, the only solution is to see such attitudes as sins. Once they are acknowledged, they can be confessed to God. It is a matter of being transparent and coming clean about thoughts, desires, and attitudes that can easily hide in your heart.

Once you choose to come clean each day before God, you can then begin to live a life that is continually open to Him. From the moment you arise in the morning until you go to sleep at night, you set yourself to an attitude of teachability and flexibility. That means God can redirect your life, teach you new insights, and reveal to you any unresolved sins in your heart. It means that you are ever ready to confess sin, change your attitude, and act on genuine needs as they arise. It sets the stage for living a life of forgiveness before God and in relationship with others.

YOUR NEED OF FORGIVENESS

Each of us is born with a sinful nature that opposes the will of God. As we grow into our childhood years, the old selfish nature becomes very obvious. That is why you may react with anger or even bitterness to someone who has betrayed or hurt you. There are many—including many professing Christians—who have allowed a spirit or attitude of unforgiveness to control them. Like an addiction, they cannot break free of its power. Once your mind allows settled thoughts of being unfairly treated or hurt, your whole body and being reacts negatively to the presence of the person who hurt you. The mere mention of his or her name can cause you stress, severe headaches, or sickness. Marriages have ceased to grow, children have been led down the wrong paths, and organizations and churches have become stagnant—producing shallow individuals who react rather respond to changing circumstances. A lack of forgiveness produces a corrupt society, which leads to little of lasting value.

But what can you do? It is impossible to eliminate deep roots of anger and bitterness on your own. The Bible has a word (*orge*) for a deep-seated anger which leads to thoughts of revenge—an attitude developed over a period of time that is not easily removed (James 1:20). The answer is to seek the help of the Lord. Only God can enter your heart, change it, transform it, and orient it toward worshipping Him and to giving your life in service to others. When King David of Israel realized his need of forgiveness, he asked the Lord for forgiveness. When he fully received God's forgiveness, his own transformed heart and life communicated forgiveness to those around him. An honest heart, a purified heart, and a

116

joyful heart lead to a **ministering heart** (Psalm 51:6-13). Like David, recognize that it is only by His amazing grace that you can please God. Thank Him for His unfailing covenant love that is ultimately expressed through Jesus on the cross. Ask Him to give you a new, clean, purified, joyful, and willing heart. When the Lord has delivered you from the addictive clutches of sinful anger and resentment, devote your life by helping set others free.

LIVING A LIFE OF FORGIVENESS

During the 1990s, when South Africa's Truth and Reconciliation Commission was conducting inquiries, a black South African woman was asked to decide the fate of a white police officer. Astounding evidence was gathered about this man who, along with others, was accused of killing her husband and son several years earlier. Her husband had been taken, tied up, and burned to death while this officer and his friends were partying. Sometime later, they came for her son, who met a similar fate. The crimes were gruesome and displayed signs of cold calculating deliberateness with no signs of compassion or remorse.

By normal human standards, this widowed woman had every right to urge the torture and death of this man by the same methods he used against her family. She could have been seething with resentment and unforgiveness. Amazingly, she responded in the opposite way. She responded by saying that she had three requests. First, she wanted him to take her to the scene of her husband's ashes so that she could give him a decent burial. Second, she forgave him of all his crimes just as God would forgive him (*if* he would accept God's forgiveness) Third, she asked that he be willing to go the ghetto where she lived so that she could act as a mother to him, because she still had lots of love to give. It was reported that the white officer was so shocked by this love and forgiving spirit that he fainted in the courtroom. Witnesses began to sing John Newton's hymn, *Amazing Grace*.

In forgiving that man, the South African woman practiced the pattern of forgiveness taught in the story of Jesus (Matthew 18:21-35). In this parable, a servant owed an enormous amount of money—10,000 talents to his master, the king. This may have been more than ten times what Rome would collect in that whole region. His debt would have been millions of dollars in today's currency. Because he could not hope to repay that debt, his own family was in danger and he was in a desperate state. There was no hope for him—except an urgent appeal to the king.

Falling down on his knees, the servant displayed the sign of deep humility. He promised to pay back his whole debt, but he and the king knew that he could never have done so on his own. In response to the servant's confession and repentance, the king gave an incredible response. He extended forgiveness to this desperate man through three essential actions:

1. "He took pity on him"—**to forgive is to experience and express compassion for the other person.**
2. He "cancelled the debt"—**to forgive is to cancel the debt of another and pay the cost yourself.**
3. He "let him go"—**to forgive is to set the other person free.** (Matthew 18:27)

The phrase "to take pity" refers to the gut feeling one has for another. It means that the king deeply identified with the plight of this servant. He put himself on the level of that man. He felt the pain and struggle of that man—feeling empathy for him in the deepest part of his heart. In his mind, the king was already **lifting** the burden of the servant. When you forgive, you do not add to the burden of another. You lift the burden of the other person by your attitude and outward response—just as the king in the parable of Jesus.

Then the king in the story "canceled the debt." Because the servant could never pay and rescue himself, the king paid the cost of his debt. Now the servant owed nothing! Jesus is teaching that forgiveness is like this action. When you forgive, you are willing to pay the price of reconciliation. You do not wait for the other person to respond. Even if they have hurt or betrayed you, you need to be willing to pay the price *for* them. Humble yourself at the cost of your pride and bruised ego. You cannot be responsible for the response of the other person, but you can be one of God's *intentional encouragers* and go the extra mile to "pay their debt." In doing so, you will demonstrate the greatness of God's grace and love. Others will clearly see in you God's **majesty in motion!** Forgiveness is not practiced because the other person deserves it, but because God freely offers His amazing forgiveness to us and cancels our sin debt through Jesus, the Savior.

If you cannot forgive another person, you have not fully received and accepted God's forgiveness in your own heart. Only a fully forgiven person who is living in the freedom of that experience can truly express that forgiveness to everyone he meets.

In the parable of Jesus, the man who is forgiven by the king, his master, is expected to extend forgiveness to those who owe money to him. But what does he do? When he meets one of his fellow workers who owes him a very small amount, he threatens to choke him unless he pays up immediately (Matthew 18:28). He is accountable for his actions and is called before the king, who had been so sacrificially generous to him. The servant is reminded of his awful sin—refusing to give to others what he himself had received from the Master. In judgment, the servant is punished.

The ending of this story is complete freedom from bondage. The phrase "let him go" has the same root meaning as the word Jesus used when he raised Lazarus from the dead. Loose him (*"Take off the grave clothes"*) and let him go! (John 11:44) The phrase can also mean to set free from bondage to live as God designed you to be. When you are resentful of another person, you "bind" him up in your mind. You want the worst for him. You don't want him to live free. Both you and the other person then live in a kind of prison, a bondage or slavery to the wrong master—to sin, Satan, to the fruits of unresolved anger and deepening roots of bitterness. But when you are willing to **release the offending person to God and treat him or her as Jesus would, you trigger the release of both you and the offender!** The result is the healing of the mind, emotions, and body! This is the majesty of God—forgiving through you and contagiously affecting many others through the power of intentional encouragement.

Practical Steps for
Individuals and Small Groups

1. An angry, negative, unforgiving spirit can control you like an addiction. The selfish nature of a sinfully flawed human being develops deep roots that cannot be dislodged without the supernatural power of God. Take time to review aspects of your past that may be hindering or crippling your capacity to live and give Christ-like encouragement.

2. Read Matthew 18:21-35. Focus on verse 30. Did the forgiven servant in the story of Jesus actually receive God's forgiveness in his heart? What is the evidence for this? What should you learn from his response?

3. Some people struggle to forgive someone else because they: 1) may have not *fully* received God's forgiveness through Jesus, and 2) have not really forgiven themselves. Does either of these factors apply to you or someone you know? What can you do to help them? (See Ephesians 4 and 5.)

4. What are the three main components of forgiveness as revealed in Matthew 18:27? What individuals close to you are in need of this threefold forgiveness? Act now to apply this in your relationship with them.

5. Note the stories on forgiveness in this chapter, including the biblical one. What price are you willing to pay for reconciliation of a person to God and with you?

CHAPTER FOURTEEN
Forgiveness Is an Attitude

In the parable on forgiveness, Jesus ends the story by teaching that each of us is just as accountable for our conduct as the forgiven servant. He was punished for not giving to others what he had so graciously received from his master. Jesus said, *"This is how my heavenly Father will treat each of you unless you forgive your brother from your heart"* (Matthew 18:35).

As a disciple of Jesus, Peter thought that he knew about forgiveness. He had come to Jesus to ask how many times he should forgive a brother. In response, Jesus told the story of the king and the forgiven servant. Peter had thought that forgiving someone seven times was a really generous act. After all, Jewish leaders taught about forgiving three times.

Jesus declared that Peter needed to forgive seventy-seven times. He meant that forgiving is a continuous way of life (Matthew 18:21-35). There should be no limit to forgiveness. The Apostle Paul reminded the Corinthians that when love is the foundation for forgiveness, one keeps no record of wrongs committed—there is no keeping score (1 Corinthians 13:5).

In developing healthy relationships connected by forgiveness, remember three crucial characteristics of forgiveness from Matthew 18:

1. Forgiveness Is an Attitude, Not an Act. When you have the spirit or attitude of forgiveness—the attitude that comes when you receive Christ the Savior in your heart—you are more motivated to forgive. The attitude comes first. If your mind is focused on pleasing God, your actions are sure to follow. Your attitude will always form, influence, and produce actions that reflect it. If you seek to please Christ, you will also seek and want to forgive in any circumstance. The act follows the attitude.

2. Forgiveness Is Unlimited, Not Limited. Allow the limitless love and patience of Christ to empower you to forgive the offender.

3. Forgiveness Is Others-Centered, Not Self-Centered. If you think of the other person and God's best for them, you will find it easier to forgive. Thinking only of yourself will magnify the hurt. Thinking of God first will help you to do the most difficult thing—forgive the other 'undeserving' person in Jesus' name! Again, Jesus is your model. Many people are familiar with John 3:16—that God sacrificially gave His very best, His only Son, Jesus, to take the penalty and judgment of a holy God for our sins—but one of the most powerful verses in the Bible speaks to the daily life of the true intentional encourager:

> We know what real love is because Christ gave up his life for us. And so we also ought to give up our lives for our Christian brothers and sisters. (1 John 3:16, NLT)

It is God's ultimate plan to include all true followers of Christ into one incredible family where each one lives fully for others. When the church age is complete and Jesus returns for His family, the idea of living sacrifice will no longer be an impossible ideal, but an awesome reality. But we must seek spiritual growth towards maturity until we begin to experience a genuine heartfelt affinity with people around us. It begins with those closest to us and extends to those whom we have just met for the first time.

> Don't forget to show hospitality to strangers, for some who have done this have entertained angels without realizing it! Don't forget about those in prison. Suffer with them as though you were there yourself. Share the sorrow of those being mistreated, as though you feel their pain in your own bodies. (Hebrews 13:2-3, NLT)

Keep God in the front of your mind (Psalm 16:8). When God is first in your mind and heart, you will find yourself thinking of the personal growth of your husband or wife, your children, and the people you meet every day. During the days of the Roman Empire, Paul taught the Christian believers at Philippi, in what is now Greece. He focused intensely on the priority of experiencing and modeling the mind or attitude of Jesus to others. Philippians 2 begins with others-centered relationships. It continues with the focus on the attitude or mind of Christ—expressed in the eternal God, the Son humbling Himself to our human level and dying for us on a cross. The chapter concludes with two vivid examples of a Christ-like attitude in real-life action.

125

TIMOTHY—MODEL OF HOW TO LIVE ENCOURAGEMENT

Timothy was a young man who deeply loved God and gave himself to meeting the needs of others and inspiring them to live a life of faithful service and integrity. At one point, the Apostle Paul admitted that he knew of no one except Timothy who was reliable enough to send to the Christians disciples at Philippi. He wrote:

> I have no one else like Timothy, who genuinely cares for your welfare. All the others care only for themselves and not for what matters to Jesus Christ. (Philippians 2:20-21, NLT)

Be a Timothy to the people in your life. Demonstrate the majesty of God wherever you go. Can the significant people in your life count on your word or promise? Are you willing to put aside some time for others when they need help? Are you willing to let go of a personal plan to help someone else if you see a genuine opportunity to honor God?

EPAPHRODITUS—MODEL OF HOW TO LIVE ENCOURAGEMENT

Paul referred to a second person who lived a life of intentional encouragement and proved it by his willingness to do whatever it took to meet the needs of others. He was known as a faithful and courageous man. In describing his work, the Apostle Paul said:

> He risked his life for the work of Christ, and he was at the point of death while trying to do for me the things you couldn't do because you were far away. (Philippians 2:30, NLT)

126

Epaphroditus demonstrated how each of us should relate to one another in our families, churches, organizations, or groups. It is a radical paradigm of servant living. He was a person who was quick to forgive and eager to encourage. He was never a loner. Instead, he sought out people to inspire, to draw closer to God. He was the ultimate team player who delighted in serving others as he ultimately served God. The Bible calls us to this when it says, "*Submit to one another out of reverence for Christ*" (Ephesians 5:21, NLT). The word 'submit' comes from two words—'to arrange' and 'under.'[xvii] It refers to your willingness to arrange or place yourself under someone else to serve them. All relationships in the church ought to be one of each person gladly willing to humble themselves and lift up another as Christ would do. It means cooperating with leaders, but yet having everyone willing to get 'their feet wet' or their 'hands dirty' to meet the needs of someone else. Gratitude would vastly increase and whining or destructive criticism would truly diminish. Submitting in the way described above would revolutionize many marriages which, in turn, would influence relationships in families, churches, and communities.

HEALTHY MARRIAGES REQUIRE TEAMWORK AND A SUBMISSIVE SERVANT-SPIRIT

God-designed marriage between a man and a woman is intended to illustrate a forgiving attitude that finds its source in the very heart of God. It is a basic building block of a healthy marriage—empowering a husband and wife to reflect intentional encouragement through gracious teamwork. Such forgiveness needs to be expressed through a submissive spirit or attitude that approaches the other spouse in a way that implies the question, "How can I serve you?"

God expects a husband and wife to be a team together that communicates the oneness of God Himself as Father, Son, and Holy Spirit. The humorous words of an unnamed person have some kernel of truth:

> In the first year of marriage, the man speaks and the woman listens. In the second year, the woman speaks and the man listens. In the third year, they both speak and the neighbors listen!

Even though the last sentence sounds funny in its context, it does have a point to make. It is true that both husband and wife ought to speak with one voice so that the neighbors get one message—the message of God's love and grace! The Bible says that God created the woman to be a "helper"—or, in the New Living Translation, a "companion" (Genesis 2:18). The word means to **make complete.** It is significant that God made the woman not from Adam's head or from his foot, but from his side. This is significant because it implies that the woman and the man are to live and serve God as partners living and walking side by side.

The importance of teamwork in marriage is made clear as the Scriptures say:

> A man leaves his father and mother and is joined to his wife, and the two are united into one. This is a great mystery, but it is an illustration of the way Christ and the church are one. (Ephesians 5:31-32, NLT)

It is no secret that God—the Father, Son, and Holy Spirit—is glorified and communicated to a needy world by a husband and wife who are growing in union with Him *and* with each other. That is one reason that the Lord Jesus expresses His desire for our growth in oneness (John 17:21).

Even though Christian husbands are called to lovingly lead in their marriages and families, both husband and wife are called to mutually serve one another in love and humility. This mutual service can only be effective as each submits to the sovereign authority of Christ: *"Submit to one another out of reverence for Christ"* (Ephesians 5:21, NLT). These words are a command to Christians to lovingly serve one another and therefore confirm the reality of Jesus Christ in their hearts. True children of God cannot help but reflect His attitude, love, and sacrificial care for anyone else in need. In the context of the Apostle Paul's message to the Christians at Ephesus, this **intentional encouraging and serving** mindset begins and flourishes first and foremost within and through the marriage relationship of husband and wife. Therefore, husbands make sure that you give intentional leadership to Christ-like teamwork in your marriage.

> In the same way, you husbands must give honor to your wives. Treat her with understanding as you live together. She may be weaker than you are, but she is your equal partner in God's gift of new life. If you don't treat her as you should, your prayer will not be heard. (1 Peter 3:7, NLT)

Marriage teamwork starts with mutual submission to the Lord Jesus. It is energized by Christ-like love for each other. It is empowered and made fruitful by a deepening prayer life together. Pray together daily. Share with each other personal insights from God's word. Make sure that there are no conflicts or wrong attitudes between you so that you can experience **power in your prayers** and live a healthy marriage that shouts Jesus to our world!

Practical Steps for Individuals and Small Groups

1. **"Forgiveness is an attitude, not an act."** Reflect on this statement and consider what you need to do to ensure that you are developing an attitude that leads to right or appropriate actions.
2. **"Forgiveness is unlimited, not limited."** What does this mean? Do you agree? How can you practice this in your daily life?
3. **"Forgiveness is others-centered, not self-centered."** Is this true? To what degree are you others-centered? How can you be fully others-centered so that they are truly encouraged by your presence, tone, words, and actions? Please carefully read Ephesians 4:32- 5:2 and Hebrews 13:2-3 as quoted in this chapter.
4. Timothy and Epaphroditus are two persons described in this chapter who faithfully demonstrated how to practice daily encouragement.
    *   List characteristics of both.
    *   List actions of both.
    *   List what you desire to **be** (characteristics) and **do** (conduct) in your daily interaction with others.
5. Reflect on the above questions and decide how you should relate to
    *   your spouse.

- your son or daughter.
- your parents.
- your co-workers.
- your fellow church member.
- your neighbor.

6. Read Ephesians 5:29-33 and 1 Peter 5:7. I believe that it was Ruth Bell Graham who said that "Marriage is a union of two good forgivers." If you are married, how forgiving are you towards your wife or husband? Does your forgiveness match the unlimited nature as defined earlier in this chapter?

7. What are indications from Genesis 2 that both husband and wife are intended by God to live and act as equal partners even though they have different roles?

8. God clearly indicates that the marriage partnership is complete with the union of a man and a woman. See Genesis 2:18. How can the marriage union reflect the majesty, nature, and the culture of God in community as "Father, Son, and Holy Spirit"?

CHAPTER FIFTEEN
Surround Sound: Communicating Appreciation

As entertainment improved with great sound technology, a key selling phrase was 'surround sound.' Suddenly, music and entertainment was no longer 'out there'; it could be all around you. You were in the music and the music was in you. Clarity, saturation—you could now be immersed in the music. Communication became complete—a total connection.

In the spiritual sphere, encouragement must not only be lived out in your life, but communicated in every facet of your life. The best way to inspire your family is to surround them with encouragement. Make every effort to speak encouragement to them even as you seek to use a variety of ways to do this.

A healthy church that seeks to honor and communicate Christ to the world is always characterized by verbal and lifestyle encouragement. God expects his people to be willing to *"speak to one another with psalms, hymns and spiritual songs"* (Ephesians 5:19). This comes as a direct result of being filled or directed by the Holy spirit of God. The word 'speaking' here means **more than saying words.** It also means to relate or communicate with others through laughter, tears, or even facial expressions. Speaking, in this sense, includes the act of crying with a person, empathizing with their pains, or rejoicing with their successes by the grace of God!

In other words, Christian disciples at Ephesus (in what is now modern-day Turkey) in the first century were called to establish a vibrant encouraging culture of 'surround sound' through sharing their hearts with one another. This would include speaking and singing psalms and songs while also sharing insights from God's written word. In communicating encouragement in a group, family, or church context, several things should be achieved:

- Inspire each person to keep their eyes and ears tuned to Jesus as the final authority.
- Lovingly serve one another as pleasing to God (Ephesians 5:21).
- Treat each one as highly valued in God's sight (Ephesians 2:10, 1 John 3:16).
- Be always alert to those who walk away from the full truth and will of God. Be willing to lovingly but firmly confront (Galatians 2:11-14).
- Motivate and challenge others to keep growing to spiritual maturity and the fullness of Jesus Christ (Ephesians 3:16-19).

- Never allow 'things' to become more important than people.

There was a family that was known for its meticulously kept house and lawn. Inside the house, most rooms were designated as normal use rooms while one room was reserved for—no one. The parents were obsessed with the living room in particular. The problem was that no one could 'live' in the living room. It was kept clean with every item precisely in place. The children faced severe punishment if that room was disturbed!

The parents communicated that the room and its 'impressions' on others were more important than the healthy development of their children. They were obsessed with outward appearances. It is good to have a clean house, but clearly reminding your children how much God loves them and how much you love them should be your first priority. We who are parents need to give three crucial gifts to our children:

1. PRESENCE

To communicate appreciation to our children, we need to make time to be with them when they need us. This means being present to cheer them in a game, to celebrate an award or a job well down, and to comfort them in troubled times. It also means being there even as a silent but supportive presence when mere talking will not help. In many families, the mother is often present, but not the father. Both parents are needed. Both need to act as Christ-like role models for the children. As a father, I may be in the same house as my children but still be emotionally absent. 'Presence' refers to being intentionally engaged with the children.

2. PRIORITY

Be very alert to the danger of neglecting your children. When our children were very young, I was guilty of becoming so busy with the families and children of others that I was neglecting my own. I was not aware of this until God got my attention through my wife Sandra. In a more positive experience, we eventually developed a process of the 'family huddle.' In our huddles, we met as a family when one of our three children came to us with a problem. We would say something like, "Okay, let's pray about this right now and let the Lord show us the way."

One of our family traditions included the Red Plate, which we used to communicate encouragement. Around the rim of this heavy plate were the words in large letters: **"YOU ARE SPECIAL TODAY."** The plate was placed on the table for our family member who had a birthday or for some other special purpose. During that meal, we would focus on that specific child or parent as our priority. It said, "You are valuable. You are our special one." It was meant to show appreciation. It was speaking loudly in symbolic fashion about our love for that family member. Now, our Red Plate is crammed with the events of encouragement and affirmation written on the back of it. It is a very special object in our family because of what it represents. Our children are grown up now, but we continue to express affirmation and encouragement to each other!

Use whatever means you have to inspire, lift up, refresh, and even challenge others so that God's purposes and grace may be fully achieved and expressed through their lives. Make sure that you connect with others through birthdays, anniversaries, achievements, bereavements, and all kinds of occasions. Develop **living traditions,** such as the Red Plate, to encourage and inspire your family members towards fulfillment of their God-given potential!

3. POSITION

By 'position,' I am referring to the giving of **direction** to your children. Don't position yourself behind your children and push them to achieve your dreams for them. Be more than a spectator in the family. Dare to grow. Maintain habits of walking with God so that you can be a moral compass, a godly father or mother who provides children who know the right direction in which to go and grow. You cannot make the decisions for them as they grow older, but you can teach them to make wise decisions. The wisest decision of all is to grow in the direction of God and not away from Him. The crime, drug culture, and 'Me' generation will have no lasting effect on those who have learned to live in the right direction. Parents, be very intentional in the way you live and gently, lovingly direct your children in the way of Jesus. Remember that none of us, including our children, can live without intentional encouragement any more than we can live without oxygen. "Encouragement is like oxygen to our souls."[xviii] We cannot live without it!

Practical Steps for Individuals and Small Groups

1. To encourage others, you need to live immersed in an atmosphere or culture of encouragement. Reflect on the contents of this book up to this point. What steps can you take to assist in the development of continuous encouragement in your home?

2. What role does the Holy Spirit play in the process and practice of encouragement in and through you? (See Ephesians 5:19)

3. Reflect on three priorities that parents ought to have for their children.

   - **Presence** -- How can you balance your time and effort for your family, work, and recreation? How healthy is the encouragement culture in your family?

   - **Priority**—What action steps should you implement to achieve and maintain your family as the most important thing—after God—in your daily schedule? If you are married with children, discuss with your spouse about actions that could be used at appropriate times to make each family member feel special. The Red Plate is just one example.

   - **Position**—You need to grow in the spiritual, social, mental, and physical aspects of your own life so that you can lead your family and others from a healthy encourager mindset and lifestyle. What can you do to arrive at that place?

4. Start by listing at least one activity for your daily calendar in each of the three priorities mentioned above.

5. Begin with more easily achievable action steps and gradually incorporate more challenging exercises to stretch yourself in your love relationship with God, in developing mental strength, emotional balance, and physical endurance. These steps will equip you to handle more difficult people and situations without you freaking out or giving up. Such personal development for you should be achieved within the context of a network of supporting friends and encouraging partners. Then you can be exhilarated rather than exhausted by intentionally encouraging others regularly.

CHAPTER SIXTEEN
The Gift That Keeps on Giving

It is possible to be and encouragement to the people that you meet. In the first century church, one man so embodied the characteristics of intentional encouragement that he was given a new name—Barnabas, which means **'son of encouragement.'** Imagine being known as a person who so personifies an encouraging spirit that your friends would give you a new name. That indicates the character of Barnabas. He was a man who truly lived out his intimate relationship with Jesus the Savior who is Himself the perfect encourager. How did Barnabas become such an encourager? No one forced him to live and act that way. There are two obvious reasons:

1. Barnabas deliberately nurtured a growing intimate faith relationship with the Lord Jesus Christ.

2. He worshipped and served God out of a community of Jesus' disciples who continuously encouraged one another as they were empowered by the Holy Spirit.

> All the believers were of one heart and
> mind, and they felt that what they owned
> was not their own; they shared every-
> thing they had. And the apostles gave
> powerful witness to the resurrection of
> the Lord Jesus, and God's great favor was
> upon them all. There was no poverty
> among them, because people who owned
> land or houses sold them and brought the
> money to the apostles to give to others in
> need. (Acts 4:32-33, NLT)

Then the Bible says that Barnabas was one of those who chose to sell some land and give all the money received from that sale to help others in need (Acts 4:36-37). Some may be wary of this as mandated socialism, but that is simply not true. Here is a situation where individuals responded to God's redemptive call on their lives and lived in harmony with and sacrificial service to others. Motivated by the in-dwelling Holy Spirit of God, they contributed to the kind of **encouraging culture** that transforms lives, marriages, churches, and work communities. Beware of any so-called 'church' or religious organization that forces or pressures you to do good works for the sole purpose of getting more converts. In the real churches of God, God and the Bible are the *only* and *final* authority and *not* the organization itself.

ESSENTIAL CHARACTERISTICS OF AN ENCOURAGING BARNABAS
It is the purpose of God that each of us should grow into Christ-likeness so that we possess and demonstrate the character traits that describe the person of Barnabas in the first century church.

Generous. Barnabas did more than give generously to others. He was a generous man. His very heart expressed generosity. He was not only willing to give to help those in need—he was will to give beyond what others expected. He was willing to pay a price, to give up something he valued, for the sake of others. He could have kept some of the money from his land sale, but he chose to give it all. That does not mean that you have to give away everything you have. God wants us to recognize that all good things come from Him, and so we should want to honor Him in the way we use them—to meet our needs and to bless others.

Good. Barnabas was called *"a good man"* (Acts 11:24, NLT). The word for good (*agathos*) refers to the character of someone. Barnabas was good because he possessed the inner character of God. He demonstrated the character and attitude of God—seeing life and people from the perspective of God because he trusted the Lord to guide his life, form his heart, and inform his thoughts. He was a good man because the good God occupied his heart.

Spiritually Mature. He was mature in a spiritual sense because he was *"full of the Holy Spirit"* (Acts 11:24, NLT). He invited the Holy Spirit to direct his life and develop the qualities of Christ in him. It is the work of the Holy Spirit to enter and reside in each genuine follower of Jesus so as to make him or her like Christ in their character. This includes developing the fruit of the Spirit, which are the personal qualities like the Lord Jesus:

> The fruit of the Spirit is love, joy, peace, patience, kindness, goodness, faithfulness, gentleness and self-control. (Galatians 5:22)

142

This is why Barnabas always sought to encourage other Christians *"to remain true to the Lord with all their hearts"* (Acts 11:23). If you will passionately pursue these qualities of Jesus for your life, you will be well on your way to living as a Barnabas encourager, positively impacting others with lasting spiritual results. Isn't this what life is really all about?

Faith-full. Barnabas was a man full of faith. In his daily living, he really did place his total trust in the hands of God. He had great confidence that God would transform the lives of all who put their trust in Christ. He was a very discerning person who sought to understand others and rejoiced when he saw the evidence of God at work in them. It took much to discourage Barnabas, whose unswerving faith in new followers of Jesus spurred them on towards spiritual maturity.

> When he arrived and saw the evidence of the grace of God [in the], he was glad and encouraged them all to remain true to the Lord with all their hearts. (Acts 11:23)

Person of Integrity. The Bible contrasts Barnabas, who lived openly and gave sacrificially, with Ananias and Sapphira, who tried to achieve the wonderful reputation of Barnabas. But they were envious of him and pretended that they were as generous as Barnabas. Their pretense misled the others in their church. They were confronted by the Apostle Peter, who reminded them that lying to the people of God also meant that they were lying to God. Barnabas was so different—he lived with transparency and complete honesty. What he revealed in public, he lived the same in private (Acts 4:36, 5:11).

Warm-hearted and empathetic. Barnabas expressed love, even for those who were unwanted by others. Saul, who was later re-named Paul, had acquired a bad reputation for persecuting Christians and trying to destroy the early church. After Saul was confronted by Jesus on the road to Damascus, he became a passionate believer and follower of Christ. But after the church leaders wanted nothing to do with Saul, Barnabas took time to understand and affirm him. Against the wishes of perhaps all the others in the group, Barnabas defended Saul and convinced them of the transformation that had taken place in his life. More than anyone else, Barnabas saw the truth about Saul and his potential.

> When [Saul] came to Jerusalem, he tried to join the disciples, but they were all afraid of him, not believing that he really was a disciple. But Barnabas took him and brought him to the apostles. He told them how Saul on his journey had seen the Lord and that the Lord had spoken to him, and how in Damascus he had preached fearlessly in the name of Jesus. (Acts 9:26-27)

Dare to be a Barnabas—a gracious follower of Jesus who always seeks to understand the hearts of others and is willing to believe in their God-given potential. This does not mean that you should accept sin and wrong attitudes in others. It does mean that you care enough to lovingly and firmly confront them for their own good and for the glory of God. Barnabas illustrated this when he confronted even the Apostle Paul over Mark, who had deserted their missionary team (Acts 15:37-39). Paul was really angry over Mark's desertion, but Barnabas saw *through* Mark's outward action and was convinced of his potential. When you believe strongly in what a person can become, you treat them according to what they can be instead of what they have done in the past.

Practical Steps for Individuals and Small Groups

1. Review the personal qualities of Barnabas. Ask yourself: Which one do I lack the most? Where do I need to grow?

2. A good suggestion is to start with "spiritual maturity," as described above. To be filled with the Holy Spirit is to experience growth in each of the above qualities. They reflect the fruit of the Spirit (the characteristics of Christ Himself).

3. Choose an accountability or encouraging partner so that you can each take steps to grow into a mature Barnabas.

4. Join a small group study to discuss and grow in your knowledge and experience of the above qualities.

5. Do you know someone who feels lonely or left out in your group, church, or organization? What can you do to help him realize his own potential?

CHAPTER SEVENTEEN
The Secret to Walking on Water

The Bible describes that incredible scene where Jesus comes towards His disciples, walking on water in the darkness of night. His sudden appearance in the murky distance not only startled them, but terrified them for a moment. They cried out in fear, thinking that he was simply a ghost. Then Jesus calmly said to them, *"Take courage! It is I. Don't be afraid"* (Matthew 14:27). Peter replies, *"Lord, if it's you… tell me to come to you on the water"* (Matthew 14:28). Jesus calls him to come and, amazingly, Peter actually walks on top of the waves! As long as Peter kept his eyes on Jesus, he stayed atop the water. But as soon as he looked down at the waves and the storm around him, he began to sink.

What was Peter's secret to walking on water? He was willing to walk into the unknown, to risk, to walk out on the edge. It was his complete trust and focus on the Lord Jesus as he truly walked on top by faith in Him. It is also true that you can walk "on top" even in difficult circumstances and lift others with you if you are willing to trust in and fix your focus on Jesus. Jesus walked on water as He focused on God the Father. He was and is one with God the Father. We can walk in victory and joy when we choose to focus and trust completely in Jesus as our Savior and Master. Each of us needs to live in oneness with Him. The secret of successful transforming encouragement is to live life and relate to others through the perspective of the Lord Jesus Christ.

1. SEE OTHERS THROUGH THE EYES OF JESUS

Jesus was constantly in touch with God the Father and succeeded in drawing to God all that the Father directed Him to reach because He **saw** them. The verb "to see" here means more than a superficial glance. This was not a shallow, surface kind of look. It means to study the crowd—to seek to understand or be acquainted with something. It means that Jesus saw through the skin to the hearts of the individual people in the crowd. Jesus saw every person through the eyes of God the Father. *"[Jesus] saw the crowds"* (Matthew 9:36).

This is really revolutionary stuff compared to the way so many people live in daily practice. We get so busy and become so frantic that we take action without our minds being engaged. How else can one explain the trampling to death of a Wal-Mart store employee in New York? Perhaps revved up by an addictive adherence to holiday sale prices, people made such a mad dash to the store that even a human life was neglected. When you live as one of God's encouragers, you are willing to live in balance and with deep sensitivity to others around you. That is only possible if you choose to make Jesus Christ your focus and not the 'me-first' culture of our world.

Many people are content with living shallow lives because they compare themselves to others instead of seeing

148

themselves in the light of God's holy and pure presence. If you look to God, you will begin to see yourself as God sees you. A deeper relationship with God leads to a deeper understanding of yourself and of others. Don't just be afraid of offending others. Be afraid of offending God, to whom all are accountable. Where is our passion to please God? Do we get so busy that we fail to see into the needy hearts of others in our churches, workplaces, and groups? To model encouragement is to model Christ in all of our relationships. Only then can we demonstrate to others the perspective, attitude, and actions of Jesus.

Seeing through the eyes of Jesus is to deeply care for others—a care that prompts immediate and timely action. Jesus tells the story of the prodigal son. In that story, He provides a picture of a father's response to a wayward son who is now returning home. In the story, it is important to note that the father of the prodigal son represents God Himself, who patiently and lovingly waits for every prodigal son and daughter who are wasting their lives apart from God. Luke describes the father's response to the sight of the repenting son:

> But while he was still a long way off, his
> father saw him and was filled with com-
> passion for him; he ran to his son, threw
> his arms around him and kissed him.
> (Luke 15:20)

When you are willing to see others as the father saw the prodigal son—with longing and compassion—you are demonstrating the mind of an intentional encourager, revealing the majesty of God in motion. Rejoice when a person chooses to put his or her faith in Christ. Do all you can to assist, help, and be a true friend by helping that person along the road to spiritual maturity.

2. EMPATHIZE WITH THE HEART OF JESUS

When we look at a crowd, we see only the crowd. When Jesus looked at a crowd, He saw not only the crowd, but all the unique individuals in need. Jesus completely identified with the people He met. He felt their joys, pains, and struggles. In empathy, you mentally place yourself inside their skin and feel what they feel—as if it were you. When you experience the ultimate spiritual heart-union with Jesus as Savior and director of your life, your heart will reflect His divine heart for your spouse, child, friend, or neighbor.

> When [Jesus] saw the crowds, he had compassion on them. (Matthew 9:36)

The word for 'compassion' means a 'gut feeling'—an alignment of His deepest feelings with those in the crowd. The persons in the crowd that day were also ones whom Jesus was willing to die for on the cross. Why did Jesus have compassion on those in the crowd? *"Because they were harassed and helpless, like sheep without a shepherd"* (Matthew 9:36). The word 'harassed' has the meaning of being loose, like limp strings on a guitar. The strings need to be strengthened, taut, in order to play good music. In addition, these people suffered from the condition of being stressed out and overwhelmed. Perhaps you feel like that at this very moment. In such a condition, you cannot live well, nor can you work well. In effect, you cannot be truly helpful to anyone else unless the "strings" on the instrument of your whole being can be fixed, renewed, and strengthened.

150

In the mind of Jesus, the persons in the crowd were like sheep without a shepherd. Like gerbils in a cage, they were spinning around in their daily lives, but not really accomplishing anything of lasting value. Even more importantly, they were not going in the right direction. They needed the sure direction of Jesus, who offered to be their spiritual shepherd and provide unfailing direction in their lives. Take time to start your day with the Great Shepherd, the Lord Jesus Christ. Contented sheep totally trust the shepherd who they always know will lead them to green pastures. Face each day with unshakable confidence by meeting with the Lord Jesus in gratitude and praise. Understand that He always walks ahead of you. Whatever your day may bring, you can face it and deal with it because He is there to lead, guide, and empower—giving you wisdom for the next challenge.

Ask God to help you identify with specific persons around you who feel stressed out, rudderless, and in desperate need of a spiritual compass to lead them in the right direction. Put yourself in their shoes as Jesus does. With sensitivity and skill, inspire them to place their destiny and present needs in God's hands. Be willing to be there for them by praying, helping, and assisting them in joining a small group of committed Christians who truly love Jesus. Like "walking on water," or accomplishing the impossible, the lasting transformation of others can only happen when you see them, understand them, and treat them as Jesus Himself would.

Practical Steps for Individuals and Small Groups

1. Consider the qualities of Peter and the reasons why he, among all of us flawed human beings, was able to walk on water (Matthew 22:25-29). As you list these qualities, reflect on how they can help you to encourage those closest to you.

2. Peter made the most of his circumstances that night. Facing deep stormy waters, he sought the help of the Lord Jesus to help him walk on the water. Think about someone in your family, town, group, or workplace who is facing deep waters at this time. What actions can you take to encourage and help them to rise above their struggle instead of sinking in its depths?

3. When Peter took his eyes off Jesus, he shifted his focus and diluted his faith (Matthew 22:30-31). How effective is faith (in Jesus) in ministering to a discouraged person over an extensive period of time?

4. What are the practical results for others when you view them from the perspective of Jesus?

5. What is the connection between Jesus' intimacy with God the Father and the way in which He saw other people?

6. Every encourager empathizes with others. How can this attitude for needy persons mold and influence your practical response to them?

CHAPTER EIGHTEEN
A Duet Performance

Have you ever listened to or watched the performance of two pianists playing in unison? Those who do it well easily capture the full attention of their audience. They play as if they were one person. In the same way, when you are willing to work in full obedience to and in complete cooperation with God, others will readily recognize the encouraging work of God through you. Be an intentional encourager as one of **God's partners** (2 Corinthians 6:1). Urging Christians at Corinth to live and serve others in total sync with God, the Apostle Paul wrote:

> We are Christ's ambassadors, and God is using us to speak to you. We urge you, as though Christ himself were here pleading with you, 'Be reconciled to God!' (2 Corinthians 5:20)

Jesus models continuous encouragement for us by *always* thinking, speaking, and acting in total synchronization with the work of God the Father (John 7:16, 10:30). It is true that Jesus struggled to obey God the Father as He experienced the cumulative weight of all our sins upon Him just before he was crucified on the Cross. Yet, the ultimate decision was complete obedience to the will of God the Father: *"Not my will, but yours be done"* (Luke 22:42).

PRAY WITH THE PERSPECTIVE OF JESUS

The vital, dynamic link of Jesus with God the Father was prayer. It is not surprising then that He commands us to pray as He prayed. The focus of the prayers of Jesus was for others—for you and me. It should be the same for us.

> Then he said to his disciples, "The harvest is plentiful but the workers are few. Ask the Lord of the harvest, therefore, to send out workers into his harvest field." (Matthew 9:37-38)

The verb 'ask' means more than simply speaking words. It means to plead, to ask with intensity of care and concern. It is to call to God with a deep intensity of mind, heart, and emotion. To ask here is to pray for someone you know who needs our Savior, or who is struggling with an addiction, loneliness, or a broken relationship. Jesus urged His disciples to pray fervently for God, who is the Lord or master of the spiritual harvest, to send more workers to people who are hungry for the God of truth and for the truth of God. By His truth, they can be set free. Pleading or fervent praying describes what Jesus does for us on a daily basis.

> Therefore [Jesus] is able to save completely those who come to God through him, because he always lives to intercede for them. (Hebrews 7:25)

Ask, plead with the Lord of the harvest for workers in the spiritual harvest. Jesus joins with you to pray passionately to God our Father in calling more workers to work in God's spiritual harvest. Why do I say *our Father?* Jesus makes it clear in His words to Mary *after* His death and resurrection:

> Go instead to my brothers and tell them,
> "I am returning to my Father and your Fa-
> ther, to my God and your God." (John
> 20:17)

Through His death and resurrection, Jesus destroyed all remaining barriers between real believers in Christ and God Himself. Now every time we sincerely and in faith approach God in Jesus name, we do so in sync with the Lord Jesus. You and the Lord pray as a *holy duet* before the Father in heaven!

Imagine what can be accomplished through your life if you are willing to be and to live as an intentional encouraging agent of God in your marriage, family, church, and workplace. This truth should motivate you with much greater passion to pray for someone and everyone, to seek the Lord in all situations with great confidence that His will can be accomplished through you! The Bible describes the beautiful scene where Abraham pleads with God for an extended period of time for the sparing of the people of Sodom from God's judgment (Genesis 18:16-33). In the scene described, Abraham is seen carrying on an intense conversation with the Lord. Why was he so concerned about the people of Sodom? Abraham really cared about them. Abraham had a genuine love in his heart for the destiny of Sodom's citizens. It was a love that confirmed his righteousness, or right standing, before God. God listened to Abraham because Abraham fully believed Him and lived for Him by faith.

To be an intentional encourager who can have a transformative effect on others, you ought to grow in the faith, love, and righteousness of Abraham. Like him, you need a resolute faith in God and in people. You need the same desire to believe in the real value of others—enough to pour out your heart in sustained prayer for them. The spiritual battle for the ultimate destiny of a human being is fierce and requires nothing less than exhaustive prayer. To win in a spiritual battle requires us to plead before God the Father with the mind, faith, and love of Christ. This is the kind of prayer that characterized Paul when he wrote to the Roman followers:

> I have great sorrow and unceasing anguish in my heart. For I could wish that I myself were cursed and cut off from Christ for the sake of my brothers, those of my own race, the people of Israel. (Romans 9:2-4)

God created you to inspire others in fully achieving their God-given potential. You are meant to be God's holy anointed representative to challenge, encourage, and lead others to become passionate and faithful followers of Jesus in the world. But you need to pay the price in prayer to the Lord on their behalf. If you are willing to advance this far in intentionally praying for others, God will enable you to pray powerfully by His Holy Spirit, who enters and lives in the heart of every genuine Christian.

> For we don't even know what we should pray for, nor how we should pray. But the Holy Spirit prays for us with groanings that cannot be expressed in words. And

156

the Father who knows all hearts knows what the Spirit is saying, for the Spirit pleads for us believers in harmony with God's own will. (Romans 8:26-27)

LIVING LIKE AN AIR TRAFFIC CONTROLLER

In the control tower at all major airports are individuals whose responsibility it is to monitor all aircraft involved in flight on or near that airport. They are on alert at all times so that they can guide or direct each aircraft in its proper path. The controller works with a focus not on himself, but for the safety and well-being of others. In the spiritual realm, you are called by God not to focus on yourself, but to live for the good of others and the glory of God. You are called to live with a high degree of spiritual health and alertness, focusing on directing others as you desire God's best for their lives.

OUR DIVINE MODEL IS JESUS

Jesus came to our world not for Himself, but for us. In the birth announcement in Matthew, it was stated that the very name 'Jesus' meant that He came to save his people from their sins (Matthew 1:21). At twelve years of age, Jesus was fully conscious of His role to serve others—wanting to do the will of God the Father (Luke 2:49). When Jesus found the original disciples arguing over who would be the greatest in God's kingdom, Jesus reminded them of His purpose—to serve others.

Whoever wants to be a leader among you must be your servant... For even I, the Son of Man, came here not to be served but to serve others, and to give my life as a ransom for many. (Mark 10:43, 45)

Jesus has given us an example of serving others with love and compassion (John 13:15). Whatever it takes to help another to her feet and set her on the road to recovery and health—*that is our calling and awesome privilege.* This should not come as a surprise us, since another name for the Holy Spirit is *'Paracletes'*—translated as exhorter, comforter, or **encourager.**[xix] This Greek term is actually the result of two smaller words meaning 'to come alongside' and 'to call.' Jesus resides in every Christian by the Holy Spirit. That means Jesus, the Holy Divine perfect encourager, lives in you and empowers you to minister to others by truly encouraging them. Like an air traffic controller, you live and stand on guard for others. But as a believer in Christ, you have access to the unlimited power and grace of God. What a privilege! What possibilities!

Practical Steps for
Individuals and Small Groups

1. To develop your life so that it continuously strengthens, inspires, and comes alongside others requires more than your own resources. The awesome grace and power of God is needed. Read 1 Corinthians 3:9 and 2 Corinthians 6:1. From the words and context of these passages, develop a plan of spiritual disciplines as the next step in becoming God's agent to connect God's power with the person's need.

2. What does the word 'ask' in Matthew 9:37-38 mean? Are you willing to ask or pray as Jesus did?

3. Hebrews 7:25 was quoted in this chapter about Jesus' role in interceding for us. How should the role of Jesus in praying fervently for you influence and shape your prayer for your spouse, child, parent, friend, or co-worker?

4. Abraham and Paul are included in this chapter as models of prayer intercessors. Are you willing to pay the necessary price in prayer, just as they were? Consider the power each of them had with God because of their eagerness to seek Him for others. What difference would it make in your prayer and influence towards others in serious need of inspiration and encouragement?

5. Jesus came to **serve**. Humble, loving service from your heart accomplishes far more in the life of another than arrogant, proud 'assistance' driven by ego and selfish reasons. How willing are you to serve according to a person's need and not according to your own personal agenda?

CHAPTER NINETEEN
Turning Visitors into Lasting Friends

In a fast-paced, self-centered world, it is a real challenge for many visitors to feel fully accepted and encouraged in homes, groups, organizations, or even Christian churches! Many professing followers of Jesus allow themselves to be too involved in the frantic pursuit of money, power, position, and privilege. It's no wonder, then, that some who visit a home, group, or church may feel ignored even by the people who invited them. Guests need to see that deep in your heart, you really care about their needs and how they feel. How sensitive are you to visitors? Do you actually invite outside individuals into your home? What you do at home influences and shapes what you do towards others in your neighborhood, workplace, or church.

DEVELOPING A CULTURE OF HOSPITALITY

The word 'hospitality' includes the meaning of love for or towards strangers. First time visitors to your home or church and new employees in your workplace obviously qualify as strangers. If you are a genuine follower and disciple of Jesus, you will want to build relational bridges with such strangers. If or when God leads you to invite them into your church or home, how prepared are you to see them commit themselves to faith in Jesus as Savior and director of their lives? Are you committed to see them grow into the best life God has for them?

So what can you do to make a stranger feel at home in your presence? Provide them with at least two vital gifts: friendship and freedom.

Teacher and writer Henri Nouwen notes that the German word for hospitality (*gastfreundschaf*) means 'friendship for the guest.'[xx] Regardless of what the visitor or guest can do for you, you need to be there for him or her. Let your visitor know that you want the best for them and that you are willing to go out of your way to help them, if necessary. Be kind and generous while being firm and helping the visitor to be accountable for his or her own actions and conduct. Your goal is to facilitate her growth into a fully alive human being who can fully reveal the glory of God to the world. Commit yourself to an offer of help and encouragement, even if the guest or visitor does not respond in kind to you. Your conduct connects not to the response of your guest but arises directly out of your own growing relationship to the Lord Himself.

Nouwen also mentions that the Dutch word for hospitality means 'freedom of the guest.'[xxi] Your intention here is to offer your visitor the freedom to be themselves, even if their beliefs or values are different from yours. As a Christian who is a direct ambassador for Christ, you want God to be at work in the heart of the visitor. It is God who can change the life of another for the better. It is not your responsibility to do this.

Pray in your heart for your visitor even as you offer them the freedom to relax, listen, learn, talk, and interact with you. Prayerfully allow God to surround their visit in a context of Christ-like love and joy without the sense that you are manipulating the occasion for your own purposes.

It has been my privilege to stay in the home of my cousin Dom and his wife Audrey. They intentionally encourage everyone who visits with them to feel at home. Staying with them is like visiting a high-end resort, except with lots of love, overflowing generosity, and deep respect for all who visit.

On one of my visits, a man and his wife stayed there while he received a check-up following serious surgery. The couple was deeply grateful. On another visit, I met another family who were staying there after fire destroyed their apartment. They were welcomed, supported, and given the freedom to stay until they found another place to live. It is obvious that visitors to the home of Dom and Audrey experienced encouragement, refreshment, and healing space without feeling any pressure to conform to the expectations of their hosts.

ENTERTAINING STRANGERS

There is a wonderful true story told about the response of that great father of the Jewish people, Abraham. It is a beautiful human model for us to follow in entertaining and welcoming visitors!

> One day about noon, as Abraham was sitting at the entrance to his tent, he suddenly noticed three men standing nearby. He got up and ran to meet them, welcom-

ing them by bowing low to the ground. "My lord," he said, " if it pleases you, stop here for a while. Rest in the shade of this tree while my servants get some water to wash your feet. Let me prepare some food to refresh you. Please stay awhile before continuing on your journey."

"All right," they said. "Do as you have said."

So Abraham ran back to the tent and said to Sarah, "Quick! Get three measures of your best flour and bake some bread."

Then Abraham ran out to the herd and chose a fat calf and told a servant to hurry and butcher it. When the food was ready, he took some cheese curds and milk and the roasted meat, and he served it to the men. As they ate Abraham waited on them there beneath the trees. (Genesis 18:1-8, NLT)

The interaction between Abraham and the visitors reveals **five essential qualities of an intentional encourager.**

1. Sensitivity. Abraham was sensitive to people other than himself. Whether in labor or in leisure, many persons focus on themselves and the pursuit of their own pleasure. The presence of visitors does not easily stir them to action. But Abraham was alert to other people and to their needs. He was others-centered. The quick response was evidence that this was a man with a deep concern for noticing, welcoming, and caring for others. Sensitivity is paired with *compassion.* Abraham showed this when he acted to determine their needs. Were they weary from a long trip? Were they in need of food or friendship? As one of God's intentional encouragers, he would think of such things and sought to help as best as he could. It was a classic case of the love and grace of God—the majesty of God—at work in one of His servants!

2. Proactivity. As soon as Abraham saw the visitors, *"he got up and ran to meet them"* (Genesis 18:2, NLT). God would do the same thing. Jesus told the story of a father who ran to meet his wayward son as soon as he saw him returning (Luke 15:20). The father was so overjoyed by the son's return that he could not wait to embrace him. Jesus teaches us of the amazing love God has for you and me. It is demonstrated in Abraham's response to his visitors. He did not wait for the visitors to come to him. He acted first—he was being proactive! God's proactive love and grace is clearly displayed here in the person of Abraham.

When you see a visitor, be proactive. Reach out to a stranger in your church—a new neighbor or a new employee at your place of work. Be alert to the prompting of God to invite a visitor to your home. Be quick to make them feel wanted and valued, encouraging them to consider the amazing love and gift of God in the person of Jesus Christ! There is no greater gift that you can offer them.

3. Humility. Abraham was *"welcoming them by bowing low to the ground"* (Genesis 18:2, NLT). The posture of bowing low to the ground points to a humble attitude. There was no arrogance here. It was not about him. It was about the visitors. He was careful not to discourage them. He truly wanted to meet any needs they may have had. The attitude displayed confirms that Abraham was really approaching them, asking "How can I help you?" Your attitude should also be the same. After all, each follower of Jesus is called to live and express the attitude or mind of Christ Jesus. Humility and a serving spirit toward visitors is a crucial part of our Savior's attitude (Philippians 2:5,8). It is a part of communicating the majesty of God to others. This does not mean that you should allow yourself to be used or abused by greedy or manipulative visitors. No, of course not. But when you are in tune with the leading of God's Holy Spirit in your life, you ought to more easily discern between those in genuine need and those who prey on kind people.

4. Grace. Abraham displayed graciousness to his visitors. He was careful not to overpower them. I have seen greeters in churches and salespersons in stores aggressively pursue visitors or shoppers—overwhelming and pressuring them. The result is that the person may not want to return to such a church or store. They need time and space to make up their own minds. God gave each person an ability to make choices. You need to let them make a choice on their own. You should *make it your priority* to provide an affirming encouraging *culture* so that they can make the right decision. Be friendly and helpful, but give then space and the freedom to make it on their own. "My Lord," as Abraham uses it, is a term of a willingness to serve someone. "If it pleases you" communicates to them that you deeply respect them and their ability to decide. In our contemporary context, it means that we should communicate our eagerness to meet the needs of our visitors and be respectful of others.

5. Sacrifice. There is a familiar saying—"People don't care how much you know until they know how much you care!" Abraham showed how much he cared about his visitors. He wanted to get food to refresh them. But notice that he did not give his visitors leftover food. He ran to his wife, Sarah. He says, *"Quick! Get three measures of your best flour, and bake some bread"* (Genesis 18:6, NLT). Then he ran to the herd and chose his best calf. When you create a culture of encouragement, offer your time and your best resources—service according to the perceived needs of your visitors. Let them know that you are willing to pay a price that says to them, "You are important to God and you are important to me." Those who are committed to Christ ought to create this culture of encouragement and care by asking, "How can I pray for you?" or "How can I be of help to you?" It says that you are willing to sacrifice or give up pursuing your own interests for a time so that you can help them. They become a priority to you.

Practical Steps for Individuals and Small Groups

1. Your treatment of a visitor or newcomer at home, work, or church can make that person willing to be a lasting friend. However, before this can happen, you need to excel in love and grace towards those who are closest to you. List the five closest persons to you—e. g. a spouse, child, or best friend. Are they also the most important people in your life? How would you describe the way you regularly treat them? Is it habit or heartfelt treatment?

2. What does the word **hospitality** mean? What are the two gifts that you should offer to your visitors according to Henry Nouwen? Ask God to help you prepare ways in which you can contribute in providing these in your home, church, or working environment.

3. List the five essential qualities of an intentional encourager as illustrated by Abraham in Genesis 18:1-8. Now make another list, this one detailing the contexts in which you can expect to meet visitors or newcomers such as in:
    - Your workplace.
    - Your church.
    - Your sports team.
    - Your social club or community league.

PART FOUR

THE PRACTICE OF ENCOURAGEMENT

CHAPTER TWENTY
The Moment You Awake:
Attitude Check

Corrie ten Boom was a Dutch woman from a family who sheltered Jews from the Nazis during World War II. For her effort, she was sent to a concentration camp along with her sister Betsie. Facing immense suffering, starvation, and possible death every single day, Corrie determined to begin with a gracious attitude towards God. She had every reason, humanly speaking, to grow bitter and give up on God and life itself. But Corrie developed the determination over the years to start each day with thanks to the Lord for His grace, mercy, and love. Ultimately, she even forgave the Nazi guards who contributed to the death of her sister and caused her so much suffering! Since Corrie allowed God to deeply encourage her each day, she was able to encourage others out of a heart that overflowed with the majesty and grace of God. Do you really want to experience joy in your life today? Then be determined to start your day with gratitude and a thankful heart towards God. You can be sure that God will pour joy into your heart even in the midst of difficult circumstances. Many days will be challenging in this life for each of us. But we can count on the joy of the Lord if we are willing to gratefully accept His grace and honor Him with it at all times. Prove God in this. It is the mindset of a true encourager.

Your next step in actually practicing encouragement in your day is to offer yourself as an enthusiastic, committed disciple of Jesus. The following provides a sample prayer that you can put into your own words on a daily basis:

> In the morning, O Lord, you hear my voice; in the morning I lay my requests before you and wait in expectation. (Psalm 5:3)

Using the theme above, offer (daily) your life to God in the following three ways:

Available. From your heart, tell the Lord that you are willing to make yourself totally available for His use during the day. Following the example of Jesus, you are willing to think, say, and act in obedience with God's leading by the Holy Spirit. In God's sight, if you are not fully available for Him, you are not available at all. You then become one who effectively shuts out Jesus from being truly at home in your heart and the director of your life. But that is essential for God to use you as one of His reliable encouragers. Choose to let God take the rudder of your boat and direct you by His word and empower you by the wind of His Spirit.

Teachable. Once you have chosen to make yourself completely available to God, you need to choose a teachable spirit. I have worked with some very talented persons who were not teachable in attitude. It was difficult, if not impossible, to work with them and to accomplish anything of lasting value because they thought they "knew it all." No one else could teach them anything, they seemed to say. Here is a very important fact. Regardless of your expertise on any subject, you do not know everything about it. If you regard yourself as beyond learning more from others, you will disqualify yourself from ever working effectively in a team. David, the king, demonstrated a teachable attitude (Psalm 51:3-6). He wanted God to clean out his mind and heart and accomplish a whole new work within him and through him to others! David concludes by admitting that God desires from each of us *"a broken and contrite heart"* (Psalm 51:17). Therefore, each morning come to the Lord with a broken or open heart—admitting your helplessness and need to Him so that He can do a fresh work in you and through you to others this day. Unless you are humble in attitude and willing to grow, God will not and cannot work through you.

Usable. Then tell the Lord that you want to be usable in His service today. If you resist Him, He will bypass you for someone willing to be usable for God's purposes. This does *not* mean that you cease to be a member of His eternal family through Christ. But it does mean that you will miss the joy of serving God at that time and that you will be held accountable to Him one day for your refusal to obey Him. Don't try to understand or attempt to figure out how you can influence others for eternity. Allow the Lord to work through you. Trust Him by faith that others will be inspired, encouraged, and moved to act on the basis of what they see in you over a period of time. If you are willing to grow daily in Christ-likeness, others *will* see more and more of the character and message of Jesus through you. Be ready for God to use you today! (Acts 4:13)

A MORNING PRAYER

Heavenly Father:

Thank you for sleep and rest during the night. It is a tremendous gift to have another day in which to enjoy you and all the good things you have provided. I realize that you have chosen me as a member of your eternal family in Jesus, Your Son. I have an incredible privilege of being one of Your ambassadors to communicate your message of life through Christ (2 Corinthians 5:20). I am not my own. I have been bought with the ultimate price of my Savior's death on the cross (1 Corinthians 6:19-20). In response to your awesome grace and love for me, I now make myself available for you to do as you wish throughout this day.

Realizing my need to become like Jesus in my whole being, I seek a teachable spirit. Teach me this day so that you can teach others through me and give to them the gift of eternal life. Whatever is in store for me today, use me freely to accomplish your divine purposes by meeting specific needs in people I will meet.

In Jesus name, I pray.

Practical Steps for Individuals and Small Groups

1. As with any good thing, a culture of lasting encouragement is only possible with the proper attitude—the attitude of Jesus. Corrie ten Boom is mentioned as one normal Christian whose attitude encouraged and transformed many Jews and Gentiles alike. As you reflect on her example, ask yourself what you would do if:
   - Your plans were slowed or stopped.
   - Someone criticized you for no good reason.
   - Your life was threatened for honoring God or helping someone in need.

2. Reflect on Psalm 5:3, as stated in this chapter, and passionately seek God to help you experience and express the threefold attitude to:
   - Be Available
   - Be Teachable
   - Be Usable
   - How can you respond to God so that this threefold attitude forms and molds your conduct, conversation, and commitment daily?

3. Use the morning prayer at the end of Chapter 20 to grow the **intentional encourager's attitude** in you. You may want to write or express it in your own words.

CHAPTER TWENTY-ONE
The Day You Live:
Avoiding the Basket

Once you get off to a good start in your day, how then do you live? To be an effective encourager for God, you need to stay out of the 'basket.' Christian leader, author, and businessman Dr. John Maxwell once told a story of meeting a couple of crab fisherman on the American east coast. They explained the coverless basket by noting that one crab wouldn't let another crab climb out of the basket. Therefore a lid or cover was not needed. In other words, one crab would not let another crab go free.

In a return trip to my hometown, I observed such crab baskets. These were round baskets, which the local fishermen used for collecting the crabs on or near the shoreline. The strange thing about the baskets was that they didn't have any lids on them! They didn't need the lids because the crabs stayed in the baskets. If one crab saw another crab trying to climb out of the basket, he would pull it back down inside. All the crabs were going to stay in the basked together—no matter the final outcome.

People can so easily act like crabs. By their attitudes, words, and actions, they prevent others from living in true freedom. They put down others, discouraging them and criticizing them. It is obvious that so many don't like to see another person succeed. There is a perverse sense of reveling in the misfortunes of others. In churches and in neighborhood cafes, this is known as gossip. If you claim to follow Jesus and be one of His encouragers, you will want to avoid the attitude of the 'crab basket.'

To avoid the crab basket attitude, examine carefully the teaching of the Apostle Paul to the Galatians (Galatians 5). The situation involved certain persons who were trying to pull new Christians back into the crab basket mindset. They were insisting that certain traditions and laws were necessary for believers—that faith in Christ alone was not enough (Galatians 5:3-4). At least some of these new believers in Christ began to listen to the intruders, or Judaizers, as they were known. The Christians then tried to please the critics rather than God. They pursued acceptance from their critics by seeking to do good works as well as practice faith in Christ. They were acting like hypocrites, pretending to trust fully in God when they were actually seeking to earn the favor of the critics.

As Paul stated, tradition, rituals, and trying to earn God's favor by working your way into His presence have no value. It is only faith in Christ alone that counts. Instead of putting people down, lift them up. Be very alert to an attitude that thinks less of others.

To encourage others to stay and blossom in my workplace, group, or church:

A. I will not:

- Focus on pleasing other people.
- Act like a hypocrite (living by other's wishes but pretending to please God).
- Pursue acceptance from others (instead of from God).
- Crave the comfort zone. (Some Galatian Christians listened to and sought to please the 'crabs' because it felt easier—more comfortable to live within a box or basket of laws, rituals, and traditions than to break free into the wider world of uncertainty where living by faith is required.)

B. I will:

- Make pleasing God my priority. I want to run the good race for God (Galatians 5:7).
- Accept any challenge that comes my way. By God's grace, I will pay the price to worship the Lord and serve others in love and continually face and resist the challenge posed by my old sin nature. *"For you have been called to live in freedom—not freedom to satisfy your sinful nature, but freedom to serve one another in love"* (Galatians 5:13, NLT).
- Reject my comfort zone and inspire others to do the same. The only way that I can do this is to keep my eyes on Jesus. When I feed my old sinful selfish nature, I

want convenience and comfort for me. When I feed my new spiritual nature through faith in Christ, I desire to pay whatever price is necessary to lift, encourage, and inspire you to live a life pleasing to God!

- Eagerly seek to become a passionate follower of Jesus Christ. Excel in whatever you do for God. Whatever you do, do it passionately for the glory of God (1 Corinthians 10:31).

Think of those moments when you work in a job and have no enthusiasm for it. There are many workers who put in time without doing a job with enthusiasm or passion. Some work mainly for money or personal gain. Others work or take action in something only because they have no choice. But you have a choice to follow Jesus. It cannot be a lukewarm choice. A life of intentional encouragement is only possible in the person who chooses to passionately follow Jesus. That requires the preparation of 'counting the cost' of following Jesus as the undisputed king or director of your life (Luke 14:25-33).

As you read this section, don't be discouraged about the cost involved. Instead, ask the Lord to help you to live fully for Him in this way and trust Him to help you every day in every way. When you stumble, sin, or mess up, confess it to Him and move on by faith. In doing so, make sure that you have an **encouraging partner** or accountability person to assist you.

179

Practical Steps for Individuals and Small Groups

1. How would you describe a 'crabby' attitude? Is there evidence of a crabby attitude in you and others around you? If so, what can you do so that the necessary changes happen in you and your closest friends?

2. Read Galatians 5 and identify the troublemakers described by Paul to the Galatian Christians. What words and actions confirm their crabby attitude? How did this affect the new believers?

3. There is death inside the crab basket, but outside of it is life. To avoid a crabby attitude and its destructive results, what should you avoid or *not* do?

4. What are the four actions you should take to experience life outside of the crab basket? Which one should be most important for you as you focus at this time?

5. How can you increase your passion and heart-centered enthusiasm for God? Out of the abundance or overflow of your heart, your mouth and life speaks to others!

CHAPTER TWENTY-TWO
Like a Loon in Water

ESSENTIAL CHOICES FOR ENCOURAGING LIKE JESUS

Abeautiful bird was resting on the surface of the lake. I recognized it as a loon. A loon is not really graceful in flight, but it is excellent in or under water. One day, I was gliding along the smooth waters of Six Mile Lake in a friend's kayak. The lake is just south of Burk's Falls, Ontario. Water is safety and security for the loon. It is in water that he fully demonstrates his skills as a diver and swimmer.

I soon discovered this as the loon heard a slight noise and noticed the movement of my craft on the water. Quick as a flash, the bird dove smoothly under the water's surface. I lost sight of him and finally noticed him surfacing on the far side of the lake. Marvelously streamlined in water, the loon can move amazingly fast underwater, especially when danger threatens!

As the loon is in water, so are genuine Christians who have Christ in their hearts as Savior and Lord. If you live apart from Jesus Christ and try to live on your own wisdom and strength, you are completely vulnerable to negative and destructive persons and values. But if you are immersed in Jesus, you have the power, safety, and security from which to influence and inspire others. It is only *in* Jesus that you can demonstrate your God-given gifts, abilities, and power. The means by which you can live by encouraging like Jesus is to remain in Him, making the essential choices outlined in the Bible (Ephesians 4:17-32).

People with crabby attitudes discourage those around them, but those who have broken free of the crab basket encourage others to be the fruitful inspirational persons that God intended. If you dare to live free of the crab basket, you can much more consistently practice the encouraging life. For the Christian, when Jesus is the resident president of your life, your goal is to live *out* what you are on the inside.

Ephesians 1-3 describe what you are in Christ Jesus. Chapters 4-6 reveal how you consistently practice in behavior what you are becoming in Christ-like character. That requires what the Apostle Paul describes as taking off your dirty clothes, receiving a washing, and putting on the new clothes in Jesus (Ephesians 4:22-23). In one of my former churches, there was a dairy farmer who would come back from the fields and barn as a dirty and smelly man. Before he could rejoin his family, he had to take a shower and get cleaned so that he could attract them and not repel them. That is also true in your heart and mind. Christians are warned to reject the condition of an unbelieving mind (Ephesians 4:17-19):

1. Reject Futile Thinking. The word 'vanity' means to think (and live) without purpose, empty superficial, futile thoughts. It is thinking that is like the chaff of the grain that blows away by the wind. The prophet Isaiah described those who live without God as trusting in vanity or lies and empty

182

words. It is a chaotic, empty lifestyle. It is often illustrated in many of the channels that are watched by so many television viewers.

2. Reject Darkened Understanding. The phrase 'to darken' means to be deprived of light. A mind that is deprived of the spiritual light of God cannot see and be liberated by the truth. Beware of those who live out of a darkened mind and mindset, such as those described by the Hebrew prophet Isaiah:

> They know nothing, they understand nothing; their eyes are plastered over so they cannot see, and their minds closed so they cannot understand. No one stops to think. (Isaiah 44:18-19)

You can renew your mind and have it filled with the light of God by continually allowing Jesus to be the master and director of your thoughts. It is in God's light that we see light (Psalm 36:9).

3. Reject a hardened heart. Those who reject Jesus as Savior are described as having 'hardened their hearts.' It means a hardened encrusted state, like a callus which forms after a bone is reset. The callus may be harder and more inflexible than the original bone. The result of hard hearts is a loss of all sensitivity to any kind of sin. Reject this kind of hardened attitude that leads to what the Apostle Paul calls 'sensuality,' or a state of uncontrolled lust (Ephesians 4:19).

Instead, a real disciple (*mathetes*) is one who comes to know Christ and cultivates Christ-like character (Ephesians 4:20). Your character is developed through a series of choices that you have made all through your life. But to become like Jesus is a process. You are making daily choices that contribute either positively or negatively to your character. Someone wrote that:

> A choice made often enough becomes a habit. A habit builds a character. A character determines [your] destiny.

CHOOSE HONESTY INSTEAD OF LYING

Real encouragers are disciples of Jesus who totally reject every form of dishonesty and lying in their lives. Such encouragers *"put off falsehood and speak truthfully with his neighbor"* (Ephesians 4:25). Even Christians are tempted to be dishonest, and will do so unless they continuously reject such temptations with the power of Christ. The problem is that the old selfish and sinful nature can easily take over unless you make a conscious choice to defeat it by applying God's resources, and not your own.

Our selfish nature wants to exaggerate the truth to gain advantage or cover our conduct. It is amazing how much gossip church attendees can produce. This amounts to lying about others. It is being rude, hurtful, and usually dishonest. Have you been honest in your workplace? Polls have revealed how many healthy workers phone in sick (when they are not sick), refuse to do their best at their job, or commit unauthorized borrowing of tools from their employer. These are all forms of lying, cheating, and dishonesty. Jesus warns us not to be like the devil, who is called *"the father of lies"* (John 8:44). Media outlets, such as radio and television stations, have fulltime troubleshooters who investigate complaints of scams built on the business of lying.

In response to this, the real Christian disciple realizes that God is his or her ultimate owner and employer. Realize that you are not working for your employer alone. Therefore, you will want to work hard and give your best in every task and job. Encourage others, including fellow workers and your employer, not only by your words and actions, but also by your attitude.

Remember to examine and guard your heart. King David realized that sin starts in the heart (Psalm 51:6). Truth and honesty must take root there first. He prayed, *"Search me, O God, and know my heart"* (Psalm 139:23). If you belong to Christ by faith, be what you are. Stay close to God and allow the integrity, honesty, truth, and sincerity of God to permeate you heart and mind.

CHOOSE RIGHTEOUS ANGER OVER SINFUL ANGER

Lasting encouragement that changes others for the good requires not only honesty, but anger. Now, much of our anger is sinful anger—arising out of our own selfish desires and attitude. Anger often erupts in a person because he or she cannot get their own way, or have a goal delayed. Self-focus always leads to arrogance, frustration, and anger. I was part of a prayer meeting in a church where suddenly one of the participants lashed out in anger—because he could not get his way! In another instance, the father of a girl had tried to arrange the murder of a man who planned to marry his daughter. He was angry because she would not marry a man from their own ethnic group. The Bible explains the reason behind all this as our desires battling within us (James 4:1-3). This is the kind of anger that leads to sin and destruction, anger that gives the devil a foothold in the door of your life (Ephesians 4:27).

What then does the Bible mean when it says, *"In your anger do not sin"* (Ephesians 4:26)? This is righteous anger—anger that arises out of a right relationship with God. Jesus was angry with those who abused and misused the temple instead of viewing it as a place of worship and prayer. Because Jesus was completely in union with God the Father, He expressed the holy anger of God. Jesus expressed anger to those who opposed Him healing on the Sabbath day. These critics were more interested in their own agendas than in the life and healing of others.

When you spend time with God each day, you will develop the perspective of God about sin in any form. You will place a high value on people as God does. That includes even being angry with a person for hurting himself or herself and hindering others who need God. Even the Apostle Paul got angry with Peter for being hypocritical and misleading others (Galatians 2:11-13). There are times when you may be angry with another, or they may be angry with you. Why? The reason is that you love God and you love the other person so much that you are unwilling to see them going astray and depriving themselves of the life-giving grace of God. Encouraging includes confronting even with an anger that cause the other person to stop doing what they are doing and make a u-turn in the right direction. This is especially true when a parent confronts a child so that the child can experience the best that God has for them. If there is an argument in your marriage, make sure that you deal with it quickly. Never wait for the other spouse to act. Humble yourself and take the initiative to make things right. When the Bible warns, *"Do not let the sun go down while you are still angry"* (Ephesians 4:26), it is warning against allowing a sudden burst of anger to slowly become a deep-seated anger or bitterness.

CHOOSE GIVING INSTEAD OF STEALING

What a radical way of thinking! There are many ways to 'steal.' Some steal money from others or steal time from employers. Instead of putting in a full day's work by doing their best, they do as little as they can or take frequent breaks. They put on a sad or mad face until they are free to go home. Some live only for the time they get paid for. A poll once indicated that almost one-third of the workers who call in sick are actually healthy. That, too, is stealing. Cheating on income taxes or taking someone's ideas without authorization are also forms of stealing. God is clear about this:

> He who has been stealing must steal no longer, but must work, doing something useful with his own hands, that he may have something to share with those in need. (Ephesians 4:28)

In other words, Paul says to the Ephesians, don't work to get, but work to give! The word for 'work' here (*ergazomai*) means 'work hard to produce something.' It means to be energetic in creatively, productively making something that you can share with others who have a need. Remember, intentional encouragers do not focus on accumulating for themselves, but on producing to also meet the needs of others. Of course, this focus is in obedience to the will of God.

How many persons can you name who exemplify the principle of excelling in work for the purpose of honoring God and increasing their giving to meet the needs of others? Can you name even one?

Clarence Andrews was a normal working man until he suffered a severe heart attack. His close brush with death sparked an *amazing transformation in his life as he realized the importance of giving to those in desperate need. He dedicated his life to raising money for orphans and school-age children in Africa. Huge amounts of money were raised from others through Clarence's work for orphanages and schools in Zambia. All of this was achieved in a region where very few individuals could be considered wealthy by normal financial standards. In May 2000, Clarence received the Meritorious Service Cross, recognition by the Canadian government for his sacrificial work and giving so that poor Zambian children could have life, an education, and a future.*xxii

CHOOSE TO ENCOURAGE INSTEAD OF DISCOURAGE

The challenge to genuine followers of Jesus is very clear:

> Do not let any unwholesome talk come out of your mouths, but only what is helpful for building others up according to their needs, that it may benefit those who listen. (Ephesians 4:29)

The word for 'unwholesome' here is *sampros*, a Greek word meaning 'that which is useless or worthless,' or 'that which is hard to stomach.' It refers to superficial, empty talking which may entertain, but weakens a person's resolve for deep convictions, self-discipline, or hunger for learning. Many conversations in bars, talk shows, or church activities reveal the spiritual shallowness of the hearts of people.

It was Jesus who said:

> It is the thought-life that defiles you. For from within, out of a person's heart, come evil thoughts, sexual immorality, theft, murder, adultery, greed, wickedness, de-

188

ceit, eagerness for lustful pleasure, envy, slander, pride, and foolishness. (Mark 7:20-21, NLT)

That is why you need to guard your heart. Feed your heart and mind with the words and truth of God. Let Jesus direct your heart on a moment by moment basis and you will speak words that will lift and inspire instead of hurt and discourage.

The key to productive speech is to focus on the needs of others (Ephesians 4:29). This requires a willingness on your part to identify with the needs of the other person and to address those needs with sensitivity and grace. Choose to be a Jonathan (an encourager to David) over Saul (who sought to discourage and kill him). After a visitor stayed in a certain village, one of the residents expressed great sadness at the time of his departure. She responded, "I like me best when I'm with you." That should be the result of our conversations with people in our homes, groups, work situations, or churches. Communicate their value by the way you treat them in conversation. Use Jesus as your model (John 4).

CHOOSE FORGIVENESS INSTEAD OF RESENTMENT

Act quickly to rid yourself of all anger, self-pity, and fixation on the real and perceived wrongs of others. If you don't, deep-seated anger or bitterness will take root and will be almost impossible to dislodge. When you allow God to take up residency in your heart, it is the Holy Spirit of God who begins the long but sure process of making you like Jesus in your character and inner being. Refusal to forgive anyone grieves the Holy Spirit and interrupts your faith relationship with God (Ephesians 4:30-31).

Two actions must be taken. First, get rid of all bitterness, anger, and every form of malice. Secondly, extend forgiveness to everyone and confirm this forgiveness by being kind and compassionate toward them. The Greek word for 'forgive' has a reflexive nature. You must first forgive yourself by *fully accepting* the forgiveness of God for you. Out of your own experience of forgiveness, you can then forgive the other person, imitating what God has done for you through Jesus Christ, the Savior. The word for forgiveness in this context has the idea of favoring someone without any conditions. Your intent should be to love them as persons, but hold them accountable for their sin or wrong in any form.

Practical Steps for
Individuals and Small Groups

1. Living in a culture of intentional encouragement, and living it out toward others, requires nothing less than a complete and constant resting (by faith) in Jesus Christ. As the loon was meant for the water environment, so too were you created to be in and remain in Jesus. (See John 15:4 and Ephesians 2:10). What choices can you make to **remain** in Jesus?

2. The physical act of water baptism is meant to symbol-ize your spiritual experience of being **immersed into** Christ. Carefully read Romans 6:1-13 and see if you can identify seven key realities of being immersed in Christ.

    - Romans 6:3: The reality of a **new identity**. Your life now becomes forever identified with the Lord. Out of His love, grace, and power, you are able to contribute to a wonderful culture of en-couragement, caring, and inspiration for someone in need.

    - Romans 6:10: The reality of a **new beginning.** Your life now models the start of a brand new spiritual life in Christ. When you live constantly out of a growing faith relationship with the Sav-ior, you can provide a powerful attractive model for someone who deeply needs a new start.

- Romans 6:18-19: The reality of a **new desire.** When you are immersed in Christ Jesus, you will no longer want to seek your own pleasures first. You will increasingly want to please God and draw others into an intimate relationship with Him.

- Search Romans 6 for other realities of being in Christ. Discuss with others in your small group how you can cooperate with God to see these applied in your life and in the lives of others. Once you practice these daily, God will produce lasting fruit through you and your interaction with others (a Christ-like cultural pattern).

3. List five choices you can make to encourage others to be like Jesus (as described in this chapter).

4. Which of the above five choices is lacking in your life? How can you make the required changes?

CHAPTER TWENTY-THREE
Sustaining the Encouraging Process

Growing to be a passionate intentional encourager is one thing. Now, the incredible challenge comes in the sustaining of this vital ministry over the long haul. We live in a society of channel-surfing and high-speed internet. Focus and concentration is not highly valued except, it seems, for superficial entertainment and current fads. Real encouragement reflects the majesty of God through human beings and requires faithfulness over the long-term. This means faithfulness to God and faithfulness to 'be there' for those struggling persons, who need not only a spiritual kickstart, but a constant friend who can always be trusted. Faithfulness is a mindset, an attitude, and a way of life that is a characteristic of Jesus. It is also a visible fruit, a dynamic practical result of the presence and direction of the Spirit of Jesus or the Holy Spirit in the life of a genuine Christian.

Apart from the Bible, you can also be inspired by faithfulness modeled in nature. Bald eagles are monogamous and remain faithful to their mate until death.[xxiii] Another example is meerkats, which are small, socially supportive animals found in areas of south West Africa, such as Namibia. Meerkats have been known to lose considerable body weight so that they can look after the young of other parents and keep watch over the colony while they are feeding. They support one another and pay the necessary cost—surely an inspiration to each of us who dare to grow to real spiritual maturity as *intentional encouragers* whose lives display divine **majesty in motion!** If you diligently seek to cultivate a continuous intimate relationship with the Lord Jesus Christ, the majesty—the greatness of God—will be impacting, penetrating, and molding countless lives of people in need of real lasting life. As Henry Blackaby wrote, "God is always at work around us."[xxiv] His gracious, awesome work is really His majesty in motion as a godly culture of intentional encouragement is developed and maintained in relationship all over our world!

A **culture** of intentional encouragement is possible in your marriage, family, church, group, or workplace. It requires a pattern of interaction between persons based on love, **unconditional friendship**, honesty, integrity, sensitivity, and compassion. All of this must be balanced by the desire to continually challenge your family, friends, or coworkers to deal with past hurts, wrong conduct, and misunderstandings that may have plagued their daily lives and could threaten them at any time. Whatever a person believes or thinks, he or she needs to **experience an undeniable sense of feeling at home** in your presence.

> Flatter me and I may not believe you;
> criticize me and I may not like you;
> ignore me and I may not forgive you.
> Encourage me and I will not forget you.
> –William Arthur Ward

APPENDIX A

Jesus is the only One who can bridge the gap between sinful, flawed people and God. Foundational to this fact is that Jesus is both authentically human and infinitely God. 1 Timothy 2:5 states that *"There is one God, and one mediator between God and men, the man Christ Jesus"* (KJV). In John 1:1-3a, Jesus is identified as the 'Word.' *"In the beginning was the Word, and the Word was with God, and the Word was God... Through him all things were made."* This same 'Word' *"became flesh and made his dwelling among us. We have seen his glory, the glory of the One and Only, who came from the Father, full of grace and truth."* (John 1:14).

God is revealed in the person of Jesus Christ, who is infinite and beyond the constraints of time. To Moses, God revealed Himself as the 'I Am' God (Exodus 3:14). While in human flesh, Jesus claimed to be God when He declared, *"Before Abraham was born, I am"* (John 8:58). This is the one God revealed as Father, Son, and Holy Spirit, who is able to do infinitely more than you can think or imagine (Ephesians 3:20).

APPENDIX B
The Making of a Partner
of Intentional Encouragement

1. I will carefully nurture my daily walk with God—being mindful to filter everything through my personal calling from Christ (John 4:34; Galatians 2:20).

2. I will discipline myself to draw deeply from God's well of salvation so that I can refresh and inspire others with the empowering grace of God (Matthew 10:8; 2 Corinthians 9:8).

3. I will lovingly relate to others out of a realistic sense of who I am in Christ (Philippians 2:4; Ephesians 1: 11-12).

4. I will engage others in conversation with sensitivity and grace. Through empathy, I seek others in connecting their need with our Savior's provision (John 4:17-18).

5. I will give whatever it takes to help another find eternal life (1 Corinthians 9:19, 21).

6. Like Jonathan, I will take the risk to help someone find strength in God (1 Samuel 23:16).

Appendix C
Church Greeters:
A Frontline Ministry

Seek to understand the culture and personality of your church so that you can be truly helpful in welcoming newcomers and assisting them in feeling at home there. Know your own identity (who you are in Christ) so that your responses can be clear, confident, and helpful to all who enter each week.

Welcoming others in a church or group context requires answers to three basic questions.

1. Who Am I?

- I am a representative of God and for my church. *"We are Christ's ambassadors, and God is using us to speak to you"* (2 Corinthians 5:20, NLT).
- I am a partner in our church family. *"Through us God caused you to believe. Each of us did the work the Lord gave us. My job was to plant the seed in your hearts, and Apollos watered it, but it was God, not we, who made it grow. The ones who do the planting or water-*

ing aren't important, but God is important because he is the one who makes the seed grow. The one who plants and the one who waters work as a team with the same purpose. Yet they will be rewarded individually, according to their own hard work. We work together as partners who belong to God" (1 Corinthians 3:5-9, NLT). *"May God, who gives this patience and encouragement, help you live in complete harmony with each other—each with the attitude of Christ Jesus toward the other. Then all of you can join together with one voice, giving praise and glory to God, the Father of our Lord Jesus Christ"* (Romans 15:5-6, NLT).

- I am a friend. *"Don't forget to show hospitality to strangers"* (Hebrews 13:2, NLT). *"When God's people are in need, be the one to help them out. And get into the habit of inviting guests home for dinner or, if they need lodging, for the night"* (Romans 12:13, NLT).

Character requirements: a humble spirit (Ephesians 4:2; Romans 12:16), a willing attitude (Romans 12:13), and a servant mindset (Mark 10:43-45).

2. Why Am I Doing This?

- I believe that God has called me to this ministry. *"Lead a life worthy of your calling, for you have been called of God"* (Ephesians 4:1, NLT). *"He was glad and encouraged them all to remain true to the Lord with all their hearts"* (Acts 11:23). *"Let us encourage one another"* (Hebrews 10:25).
- I have a passion to share the mind of Christ with others. *"Be humble, thinking of others as better than yourself. Don't think only about your own affairs, but be in-*

terested in others, too" (Philippians 2:3-4, NLT). See also Philippians 2:5.

- I am committed to communicate the mission of our church. *"As each part does its own special work, it helps the other parts [members] grow, so that the whole body [church] is healthy and growing and full of love"* (Ephesians 4:16).

3. WHAT IS MY ROLE?

- Be spiritually prepared (Bible study, prayer, worship, and witness).
- Confess any known sin in my life to God.
- I seek to be flexible, loving, and sensitive to the needs of those who enter our church (Romans 12:9-10).
- I strive to earn the respect of our church so that in my role as a leader, I can truly help grow our church (Philippians 2:29).
- As people enter, I silently pray for visitors and members even as I welcome them.
- It's not about me. It's about God. If it's about God, it must be about others (2 Corinthians 8:9).

ENDNOTES

i   John Maxwell, *Ten Trade-offs Worth Making*, Vol. 11 No. 8, Injoy Life Club (San Diego: Injoy, N.D.).

ii   The term *al-lebab* appears in 2 Chronicles 32:6.

iii   W.E. Vine, *An Expository Dictionary of New Testament Words* (Old Tappan: Fleming H. Revel, 1966), 208.

iv   Lisa Arrowsmith, Canadian Press, "Artificial Organ Helps Teen's Heart to Heal." *The Globe and Mail*,   August 29, 2007.

v   *Funk and Wagnalls Desk Dictionary* (New York: Funk and Wagnalls, 1976), 391.

vi   William F. Arndt and F. Wilbur Gingrich, *A Greek-English Lexicon of the New Testament* (Chicago: University of Chicago Press, 1957), 497-8.

vii   Irwin McManus, *Seizing Your Divine Moment* (Nashville: Thomas Nelson, 2002), 34.

viii   Johann Wolfgang von Goethe. A German dramatist, novelist, poet, and scientist (1749-1832).

ix   John Maxwell, *The 360 Degree Leader* (Nashville: Thomas Nelson, 2005), 177.

x   Dan Allender, *The Healing Path* (Colorado Springs: Waterbrook Press, 1999), 201.

ENDNOTES

xi   David Roper, *Psalm 23: The Song of a Passionate Heart* (Grand Rapids: Discovery House, 1994), 12.

xi   *I'm in a Hurry (And I Don't Know Why)*. Alabama.

xii   This advice was given by a wonderful pastor-friend, Dr. Stan Hibbins.

xiii The word in the Hebrew means "cup of saturation."

xiv 1 Corinthians 12:4-11 is a reminder that God gives each follower of Christ a gift or gifts as He determines. To paraphrase Job, God can give or take away as He wills (Job 1:21).

xv   Linda Nuguyen, *Edmonton Journal*, Canwest News Services, November 14, 2008, A7.

xvi *Funk and Wagnalls Desk Dictionary* (New York: Funk and Wagnalls, 1976), 338.

xvii W.E. Vine, *An Expository Dictionary of New Testament Words* (Old Tappen, New Jersey: Fleming H. Revell, 1966), 86.

xviii From a sermon preached by Dr. T.V. Thomas at First Filipino Alliance Church, Edmonton, AB, November 23, 2008.

xix W.F. Arndt and F.W. Gingrich, *A Greek-English Lexicon of the New Testament* (Chicago: University of Chicago Press, 1957), 623.

xx   Henri Nouwen, *Reaching Out: Three Movements of the Spiritual Life* (New York: Doubleday, 1975), 51.

xxi Ibid, 51.

xxii Paul Banks, "Newfoundland Agape School Recently Completed in Africa." *The Gander Beacon*, June 18, 2001.

xxiii www.wikipidia.org/wiki/Bald_Eagle#Reproduction

xxiv Henry Blackaby, *Experiencing God* (Nashville: LifeWay Press, 1990), 15.

ABOUT THE AUTHOR

Stewart passionately seeks to encourage people everywhere through his role as author, seminar teacher, and pastor of discipleship in Edmonton, Alberta. He has pastored several churches across Canada, including Toronto and Halifax. He is a graduate of Brock University, Tyndale University College, and Bethel University in St.Paul-Minneapolis, Minnesota (where he earned his Doctor of Ministry degree). Stewart is the grateful husband of Sandra and the encouraged father of three sons, three daughters-in-law, and two granddaughters. Stewart also drinks deeply of God's encouragement in his enjoyment of cycling, hiking, and working out with others in the local YMCA gym.

Stewart welcomes your comments, questions, or invitations to speak by contacting him through his website— www.oneheartministries.ca.